Trouble
Free
TriAngles

GAYLE BONG

That Patchwork Place®

DEDICATION

TO MARK, WHO CAN HARDLY WAIT TILL
THE NEXT QUILT IS FINISHED SO HE CAN USE IT.

ACKNOWLEDGMENTS

MY SINCERE THANKS GO TO THE FOLLOWING
PEOPLE WHO MADE QUILTS, TESTED PATTERNS,
AND HELPED IN WAYS TOO NUMEROUS TO MENTION.
THEIR WORDS OF ENCOURAGEMENT AND SUPPORT
WERE ESPECIALLY APPRECIATED: LISA BONG,
LINDA BOHLING, PAT TITUS, ROSE LAUCHART,
SHIRLEY SCHARNOSKI, SALLY PARKER,
VALERIE BONHIVERT, JEANNE BLISS, SUE BONG,
LORRY TAYLOR, MARY NOVAK, PEG RIESE,
CARRIE STANEK, AND NANCY LINZ.

Trouble Free Triangles
© 1995 by Gayle Bong
That Patchwork Place, Inc., PO Box 118,
Bothell, WA 98041-0118 USA

MISSION STATEMENT

WE ARE DEDICATED TO PROVIDING QUALITY PRODUCTS
THAT ENCOURAGE CREATIVITY AND PROMOTE SELF-
ESTEEM IN OUR CUSTOMERS AND OUR EMPLOYEES.
WE STRIVE TO MAKE A DIFFERENCE
IN THE LIVES WE TOUCH.

That Patchwork Place is an employee-owned,
financially secure company.

CREDITS

Editor-in-Chief **Barbara Weiland**
Technical Editor **Laura M. Reinstatler**
Managing Editor **Greg Sharp**
Copy Editor **Liz McGehee**
Proofreader **Leslie Phillips**
Illustrator **Brian Metz**
Illustration Assistant **Lisa McKenney**
Photographer **Brent Kane**
Photography Assistant **Richard Lipshay**
Design Director **Judy Petry**
Text and Cover Designer **Amy Shayne**
Production Assistant **Claudia L'Heureux**

Library of Congress Cataloging-in-Publication Data

Bong, Gayle.
    Trouble Free Triangles / Gayle Bong.
        p.   cm.
    ISBN 1-56477-113-X
    1. Patchwork—Patterns. 2. Quilting—Patterns.
3. Triangle in art.   I. Title.
TT835.B625 1995
746.46—dc20   95-374
                                                CIP
Printed in Hong Kong
00 99 98 97 96 95   6 5 4 3 2 1

TABLE OF CONTENTS

PREFACE

I began searching for quilt designs based on the equilateral triangle while working on my first book, *Infinite Stars.* I found a few that were familiar to me: Spider Web, Smoothing Iron, Thousand Pyramids, Seven Sisters, and Tumbling Blocks. Grandmother's Flower Garden is another old favorite, not often thought of as being based on the equilateral triangle, but a hexagon, after all, is composed of six equilateral triangles. Then there were those that were less familiar—Bluebirds for Happiness, Trillium, and Sugar Loaf, to name a few.

I noticed that few of the blocks actually used a pieced triangle as the repeating design element. I did find new designs that had been based on the triangle; however, these, too, did not use a pieced triangle in the traditional sense of a repeating design element. It didn't take me long to realize that triangle block designs had largely been left unexplored. This sounded like a challenge to me. How exciting!

Quilt designers have been using the equilateral triangle more frequently in this latest quilting revival, especially now that we can rotary cut these shapes and use equilateral-triangle graph paper for designing. I began to experiment with designs that fit into a grid of equilateral triangles, using shapes I could rotary cut with the techniques I developed for *Infinite Stars.* With the triangle as my format, I then explored the different setting options for the triangle blocks. The similarities and differences between square blocks and triangle blocks soon became apparent.

I had fun playing with the blocks, discovering endless possibilities for exciting new designs. The result is my first collection of triangle block designs.

INTRODUCTION

I think Sara Nephew was right when she said there are probably as many design possibilities for the triangle as there are for the square. Sara has written six books based on equilateral triangle designs and has developed the ClearView Triangle™ ruler.

Trouble Free Triangles begins with a look at the basic equilateral triangle. By dividing the triangle into smaller units, different block patterns emerge. On pages 7–13, more than fifty block illustrations, classified by the order in which they are assembled, are followed by suggestions for designing a quilt from triangles. Tips for choosing fabric include directions for making a mock-up or a sample block to test your choices.

I hope you will read the information in the first section, regardless of whether you intend to design your own quilt. The insight you gain will ensure an understanding of the piecing and assembly techniques. While the information is not exclusive to equilateral triangle-based designs, you may learn an exciting new technique or valuable tip that will help you when working on future projects.

Complete directions are given for using the ClearView Triangle. This is the specific tool used to cut the shapes in the triangle blocks. I've also included the latest quick-piecing techniques adapted to the 60° angle. The final section provides general information for sewing the pieces and includes a few tips for working with this angle.

The pattern section includes eleven designs, arranged from easiest to most challenging.

With this book, I hope to open the doors to triangle patchwork. My wish is that you enjoy these techniques and that they become a new tradition in your quilting.

TRIANGLE PATCHWORK

DESIGNING TRIANGLE BLOCKS

Just what is an equilateral triangle? I am often asked this question when I explain my specialty in quilting. Many of us remember the term from geometry class. Although we don't need a refresher course in geometry, it would be helpful to understand the shapes we'll use when we work.

The equilateral triangle is not to be confused with the 45°/90° triangle commonly known in quilting as the half-square triangle. Each of the angles of an equilateral triangle is 60°. Each side of an equilateral triangle is identical in length.

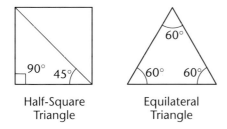

Half-Square Triangle   Equilateral Triangle

Most traditional patchwork blocks are based on a graph of squares. By working on equilateral-triangle graph paper (available at quilt shops), you can easily design triangle blocks. Working within the structure of a triangle grid, you can also use a group of related shapes that work together with the triangle. These shapes have 30°, 60°, or 120° angles. They include the diamond, half diamond, parallelogram, hexagon, triangle, half triangle, trapezoid, and gemstone.

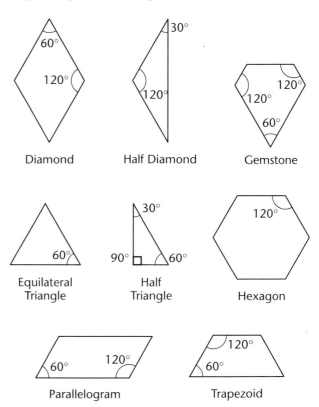

Diamond   Half Diamond   Gemstone

Equilateral Triangle   Half Triangle   Hexagon

Parallelogram   Trapezoid

I designed the corners of the triangle blocks to resemble elongated corners of traditional square blocks, as though someone pulled on one of the square corners, stretching it out of shape. This was a carry-over from *Infinite Stars* in which I transformed square blocks into diamonds using the triangle graph paper.

Using the elongated units in the corner of the triangles gives them a somewhat traditional look. With their corner units based on a traditional four-patch unit, they naturally fit into a triangle grid of six divisions on each side.

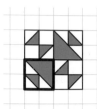 

The triangle between each corner unit can be used as a single unit or divided into smaller shapes.

Triangles used as single units   Triangles divided into smaller shapes

I further devised more blocks by rotating units, making substitutions, and altering positions of the light, medium, and dark colors. Playing with the blocks led to designs that follow other natural divisions of the triangle grid.

I discovered that triangles with internal grids made up of any number of divisions on each side can be used, although the smaller the block, the less room there is for design elements.

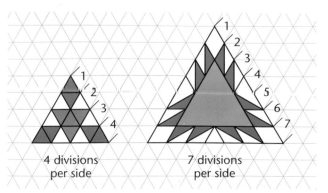

4 divisions per side   7 divisions per side

I designed larger blocks by elongating the ninepatch corner unit from a traditional block. Note how they fit into a triangle grid of 9 divisions per side.

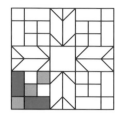

Designing from large blocks has great design potential because of the greater number of pieces available to manipulate. A larger, more complex block means that you can fill a large space with fewer total blocks than you would need if you filled the same space with small blocks. A larger block means fewer repeats of the design.

The one rule to remember for Template-Free® cutting is that the lines of the design have to intersect where the grid lines intersect.

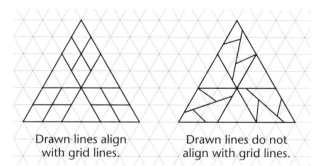

Drawn lines align with grid lines.   Drawn lines do not align with grid lines.

There is nothing tricky about sewing the triangles together. Just as in square blocks, small units are sewn together into larger units, which are then sewn into blocks. None of the designs in this book require "set-in" pieces.

There are four basic methods of constructing a triangle block. The blocks on the following page are based on an internal grid of six divisions on each side. They are classified by how they are constructed.

Method 1. Unequal halves. As its name implies, this triangle block is made up of two sections of unequal size. The top half has a diamond unit and two triangle units, and the bottom half has two diamond units and one triangle unit. The following blocks are based on this method of division.

Method 2. Hex-out. In this block, a triangle unit is added to three sides of a hexagon. Use the simpler blocks as "connector" type blocks, which are designed to be alternated with other triangle blocks for two-block quilts.

Method 3. Tri-out. These blocks begin with a plain or pieced triangle in the center, then a plain or pieced triangle is added to each side.

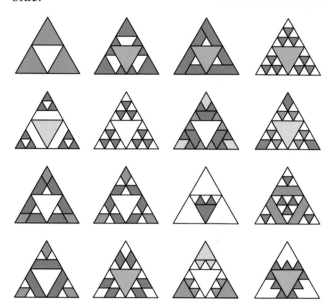

Method 4. Tri-log. Imagine a triangle Log Cabin block, and you will understand how this category is constructed. These blocks also begin with a triangle in the center. Then a trapezoid is added to each side, each one longer than the last until the block is complete. The trapezoids are usually pieced.

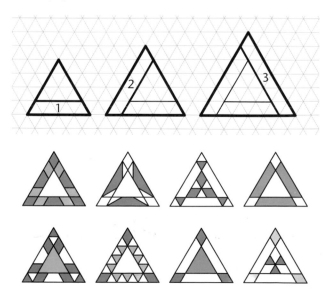

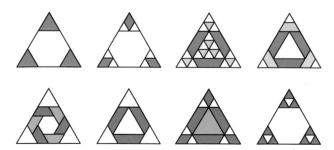

7

SETTING TRIANGLE BLOCKS

The similarities between quilts based on squares and quilts based on triangles don't end with the blocks. After designing the blocks, you must choose an arrangement or setting for them. While designing the quilts for this book, I considered all the settings common to square patchwork blocks and a few unique to triangle blocks.

Try one of the following methods for designing your own quilt using triangle blocks. Designing isn't for everyone, but it is easier than you think and it's fun. It helps to know what you like. If you don't like what you have designed on paper, you can always change it. Develop the practice of asking yourself "What don't I like about this design so far?" When you have the answer, you can begin to improve it. Drawing the design on paper is helpful for deciding when it looks complete. Cutting and pasting, erasing, and re-drawing are easier and less expensive with paper than cutting into the fabric and then deciding you don't like the setting.

A simple way to begin exploring design possibilities is to place tracing paper over existing diagrams to make changes here or there. Break a large shape into smaller units or simplify a design by combining two or more pieces into one unit to create numerous variations. Or experiment with color and alter the placement of lights, mediums, and darks.

For endless design possibilities, design your own blocks or choose and copy a few of your favorite blocks from page 7 onto equilateral-triangle graph paper. Transfer just the design lines (those lines outlining the different values or colors within each block) so you can color several variations. Make about twenty photocopies of the blocks. Cut out the blocks and arrange them, referring to the setting suggestions illustrated on the following pages, or try combining the settings.

Make multiple photocopies of each setting or color them on tracing paper placed over each setting if a photocopier is not easily accessible. By coloring on the tracing paper, you will preserve the line drawing for coloring several variations. Remember when you changed the values within one block design, how the blocks changed even though you used the same pieces to make the block? The same thing happens with a quilt design. Experiment by coloring subtle value changes from block to block or variation to variation.

You won't be able to make all your decisions from a colored-pencil sketch, but it can help when it comes to choosing fabrics. Visualizing the finished quilt is easier if the coloring resembles the fabrics. Press firmly to produce the dark fabric tones and press lightly to represent the light and medium fabric colors. Once you have chosen your fabrics, make a mock-up as suggested in "Fine-Tuning Fabric Choices" on page 15.

Probably the most common arrangement of blocks is to set them in a straight row, side by side, throughout the quilt. The side-by-side sets are more interesting if there are two colorations of the same block. The "Smoothing Iron" quilt and its variations illustrate this.

Many blocks, when turned and joined side by side, will form stars. This block has a Southwest feel.

When blocks are set side by side with the rows offset, a zigzag effect is likely to result as in "Fall Festival" below.

If the rows are offset, the blocks line up directly above one another. With the blocks stacked on top of each other, the corners do not meet to create secondary designs. Within the row, try alternating each pieced block with a plain block.

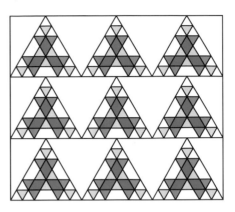

Setting the blocks with alternate plain triangles isolates the blocks, placing the focus on the block rather than the entire surface design. This lends to the appearance of an antique quilt design. Using reproduction fabrics further contributes to the look of an antique. While quilts made a century ago were often made of scraps, they were also made with a limited number of fabrics. Today we purchase "scraps" to add the variety we find so appealing—often our "best" quilts are made with these purchased scraps.

The sides of a quilt with alternate plain blocks can be finished with pieced half blocks, as in "Potluck" (page 37), or plain half blocks. "Sunday Best" (page 34) features plain half blocks at the sides of the quilt design, plus a pieced border around the edges.

Choose a quilting pattern compatible with the mood of the quilt. For example, Linda Bohling's antique look-alike scrap quilt, "Potluck," is best quilted in a grid of diamonds or an overall pattern, such as the Baptist fan. A feathered heart design is a suitable choice for the alternate plain blocks in "Sunday Best."

Try alternating plain dark blocks with pieced blocks when you want a "country-style" quilt.

Two-block quilts offer the secondary and tertiary designs I love. They often provide the illusion of movement and depth, or of layers of patchwork.

Don't overlook the simplest blocks when trying various combinations. Often, they are the best choice for the alternate block. An unpieced area in a design offers a resting space for the eyes. Choosing a busy fabric or two busy blocks may clutter the design, creating tension. Something simple may be more traditional or "restful."

"Triplicity" (page 35) combines a pieced block with a "connector" block that simply has a diamond in each corner. This design results in a soothing traditional quilt.

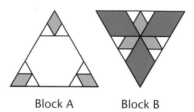

Block A   Block B

"Dancing Diamonds" (page 36) features two blocks, either of which, when alternated with any other block, creates a chain, or interlocking ring, of diamonds. This chain runs through the quilt, creating movement, but the movement is calmed by repeating the fabrics.

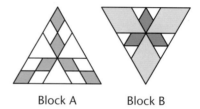

Block A   Block B

In "Magic Jewels" (page 40), two kinds of similar star blocks join to form the flower motif. Viewed as a whole, the blocks form a star.

Two-block quilts create secondary patterns where the boundaries of the blocks are disguised.

Sometimes the design can be pieced in several ways, so analyze your design to determine the best way to assemble it. There may be fewer seams if pieced one way, but there may be fun quick-piecing techniques the other way. Review the cutting section to help identify the blocks that will be easiest to piece. The illustration below shows several possibilities for piecing the blocks to make the design.

To balance the look of the quilt, use an odd number of rows. Begin and end each row with the same block. For example, start the row with Half Block A and end with Half Block A in reverse. Avoid using a whole block at one end and a half block at the other end, or using a Half Block A and a Half Block B at each end of the row. An exception to this is when you wish to make the quilt look like an antique quilt. Applying these rules to planning two-block arrangements may be a bit more challenging, but the rewards are worth the effort.

Study the block placement diagrams in the pattern section. Notice that partial blocks or units were added to the top and/or bottom edges to complete some of the designs. Other designs end with half blocks placed only along the sides. Partial blocks may be required on all the sides as well.

If you need half blocks at the edge of the quilt, you can cut only the pieces necessary for half blocks. In the illustration of the half block above right, the half triangles and half diamonds have been cut to include seam allowances. Or, make a

whole block, then cut it in half. If you do this, however, be sure to cut ¼" beyond the center line to allow for the seam allowance. The remaining portion is then unusable for the project.

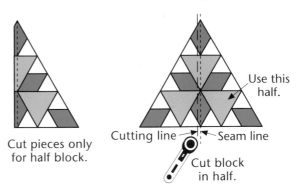

Cut pieces only for half block.

Use this half.

Cutting line — Seam line

Cut block in half.

To answer the following questions, use photocopies or tracing paper to experiment with the different looks you can achieve.

How might the edges best be finished in the illustration below? Should they be straightened up with half blocks? Should just the dark triangles be complete along the sides of the quilt? Should the triangles extend into the border? Should the top row be completed with the alternate block?

This might be a good opportunity to start at the top of the quilt with one block predominating and end at the bottom with the second block predominating. This way, the two blocks will appear to merge and overlap at the center of the quilt.

Diagonal settings, common to squares, are generally not used with equilateral triangle quilts.

11

Equilateral triangles don't have a diagonal in the same way that squares do, although I suppose the triangle blocks could be tipped if you feel a design looks better that way. I feel as if I must tilt my head when I look at these designs turned at an angle. Turn the book on its side and look at the diagrams to see what I mean.

Medallion sets are difficult because planning a pieced border on paper isn't exact (more about borders later). If you are not a quilter who plans on paper but you understand the technique of applying pieced borders, you might enjoy experimenting with a medallion set.

Not surprisingly, there are a few settings unique to triangles. Though they may be tricky to piece, probably requiring set-in seams or partial seams, they would be a worthy challenge if you're looking for something unusual.

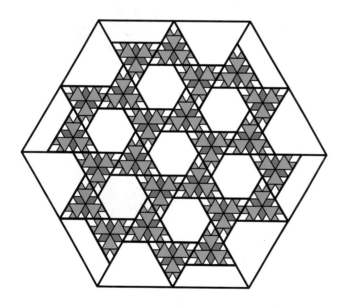

DESIGNING SASHING SETS FOR TRIANGLE BLOCKS

To tame busy blocks set side by side, sash them. Either lay the blocks out on sashing fabric to decide on sashing width or graph them first. I find that graphing a sashing set is awkward. A simple sashing design requires two rows of graphed triangles before the next row of blocks is in the correct position. This makes the sashing look too wide.

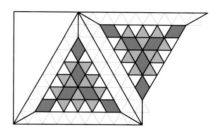

For actual quilts, use a narrower sashing for an effective design. It does not need to be the same scale as the blocks, as long as the sashing around each block is the same width. A quilt with this type of sashing requires a skilled piecer to keep the blocks evenly spaced.

I find it preferable to sash each block separately. This results in a seam down the middle of the sashing when the blocks are joined, but it can be disguised by choosing a printed fabric. Or, introduce another design element by alternating the sashing colors.

In the illustration above, twelve seams converge where the sashing strips intersect. One way to avoid this piecing challenge is to use long, narrow trapezoids, sewing them to each block, Log Cabin–style.

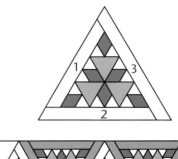

Consider using a pieced sashing. Place a sheet of tracing paper over a diagram with wide sashing and color in a few pieces to see if a pieced sashing creates an intriguing design.

CHOOSING FABRIC

Your design is finished and you are ready to start on your quilt. First you must choose your fabric. Most quilters enjoy selecting fabrics for a quilt. If you find it a chore, I suggest you begin by choosing a focus fabric. Select a multicolored print of medium to large scale, then choose fabrics that coordinate with it. When selecting the coordinating fabrics, choose a range of light-, medium-, and dark-colored fabrics. I find that this range produces the most successful quilts.

Don't be fooled into thinking your focus fabric is dark if it actually reads as a medium value. Step back ten feet and look at the fabrics you are considering. Do you see a definite distinction between them? If you don't, you are likely to lose the design.

Include a variety of sizes in the prints of the fabric you use for added interest. Don't overlook the solid-colored fabrics. They add a clean, crisp look to the quilt. Avoid one-way or directional prints, particularly for the background areas of the design.

I use strictly 100% cotton for my quilts. It is by far the most popular fabric for quilts, and with good reason. It is easiest to work with. Cotton holds a crease better than polyester blends, and it doesn't "pill" the way synthetics do.

If you have a quantity of blends in your stash, consider reserving them to use for making kids' quilts or lap quilts in which fabric is "used up" quickly. Perhaps the local quilt guild or other organization would be happy to add the fabric to their stash for service projects.

If you are unsure whether or not the fabric is a blend, you can give it the burn test. To test the fabric, cut a 2" square. Hold it with a pair of kitchen tongs over a candle or gas range. Burn about half of it. As it burns, notice whether the smoke is black or gray. Black smoke will smell like petroleum and indicates a synthetic blend fabric. Before the fabric is completely burned, extinguish the flame. Are the ashes gray? Is the burnt edge of fabric gray and ashy or crispy and black? If the burnt edge is gray and ashy, the fabric is cotton.

PREPARING FABRIC

Always launder your fabric before using it in a quilt. Washing preshrinks it and removes excess surface dye, which could transfer to other fabrics. Use warm water and a mild detergent. Completely unfold the fabric before placing it in the washer. If it is a dark fabric and you are concerned about the color running, rinse it in the sink first until the water runs clear. After prerinsing, it should still get the full treatment in the washer and dryer.

The dryer does more to shrink the fabric than the washer. Be sure to remove and fold the fabric promptly, to avoid having to iron any more than necessary. Washing and drying small quantities helps reduce the amount of wrinkling, too.

Launder quilts in cool water, but spread them upside down on a sheet on the picnic table to dry on a warm, breezy day.

Fine~Tuning Fabric Choices *fine.*

I highly recommend making a mock-up or a sample block. This is an excellent way to judge your fabric choices. I know well the disappointment in choosing the wrong fabrics. Not only is it a waste of time and money, but occasionally I've even felt it to be an embarrassment. Through experience, I have found I often use my second or third choice for at least one of the fabrics I initially chose for the quilt.

To make a mock-up, use a rotary cutter to cut the pieces without seam allowances. If you prefer templates, draw the block first on graph paper. Reduce the size to half if you are not using a printed fabric with a large scale. Iron the back side of the drawing to a fusible web, such as Wonder-Under®, then peel away the backing paper. (If your blocks are asymmetrical, iron the front side to the fusible web.)

Cut out the paper pattern pieces. Iron the pieces to the back side of your fabrics and cut them out. Arrange these on another sheet of paper and glue in place. Often, I do not cut out the background fabric but instead arrange the other pieces on a large piece of background fabric.

Making a sample block helps me determine if the pattern chosen is suitable for my abilities. Though a challenge is a good way to develop my skills, I don't want to get in over my head. I don't make sample blocks for scrap quilts or very small quilts, or for the simplest block patterns.

While sewing the sample block, work out the directions to press seam allowances. After the quilt top is finished, use the sample blocks for choosing the quilting designs. (This is a good opportunity to test how easily the pencil marks can be removed from the actual fabrics used in the quilt.) Consider starting a collection of sample blocks of all your projects as a keepsake of the quilts you give as gifts.

Using a Design Wall

A design wall offers a great advantage when evaluating the design in progress. My flannel-covered design wall is made of insulation board purchased from the lumberyard and doubles as a bulletin board.

A design wall provides the best view of a project because you see the design straight ahead of you, instead of at an angle when you look at it on a table or floor. You can stand up to work rather than getting down on your hands and knees. A design wall keeps the project off the floor and out of the way of family members, and, if you can get far enough away from it, it's a great place to take photographs of your work.

A design wall is easy to use. Simply press your fabric pieces or blocks against it. The fuzzy surface grips the fabric, so pinning is not necessary. Rearranging pieces is easier because they don't slide out of place and you don't need to repin. The rule to remember when taking a design off the flannel wall is to only remove what you will remember how to replace.

A permanent design wall is ideal; if you do a lot of quilting, you'll wonder how you got along without it. If you don't have room for a permanent design wall, use a wall where you can remove a picture or two and temporarily hang some white flannel. Just place a few hooks in the ceiling and sew corresponding buttonholes along the edge of the flannel. Felt or quilt batting are good choices, too, and can be thumbtacked or stapled directly to the wall.

60°-Angle Rotary Cutting

Tools

Rotary Cutter. For many quilters, the rotary cutter has all but replaced the use of scissors in making patchwork quilts. Rotary cutting speeds up the quiltmaking process by making the cutting faster. Exercise care when cutting and sewing and you will save time in the long run. It is amazing how much time can be spent ripping, recutting, and fudging!

Make sure the blade for your rotary cutter is sharp. Think of it as a round razor blade. Replace the blade when it begins to skip repeatedly and requires more pressure to cut through four layers of fabric. Clean and add a drop of oil between the blade and the guard to extend its usefulness.

I like the mid-size cutter (1¾"-diameter blade) for most cutting because it is more comfortable in my hand. The small cutter (1⅛"-diameter blade) is great for cutting small pieces, such as those used in miniatures and strip-pieced half diamonds.

Cutting Mat. Always use a cutting mat when using a rotary cutter. The blade will damage any other surface, and the mat protects the blade from quickly becoming dull and needing to be replaced. I prefer a large mat because the fabric fits easily, requiring a minimum of shifting and readjusting before cutting. When not in use, store the mat flat. If your storage and work spaces are limited, a smaller mat may be a good choice for you.

Small mats are excellent to take to classes. You will find it easier to use the small mats at class if you make the initial fabric-straightening cut on a large mat at home. (See page 17.) An advantage of a small mat is that you can move the fabric into cutting position by turning the mat; repositioning a small mat requires less room on the work surface.

Rotary-Cutting Guides. Most cutting can be accomplished by using a long straight-edge ruler marked with a 60° angle, but I find such rulers confusing. Although there are several 60° triangles on the market, they are each marked differently, and the patterns in this book may not work with all of them.

In addition to a 24"-long, ⅛"-thick acrylic quilter's ruler, I recommend using the ClearView Triangle by Sara Nephew. The directions in this book were written with this tool in mind. This specialized triangle ruler allows quick and accurate cutting and comes in three sizes. I prefer the 8" for most cutting. The 12" triangle is great for accurately cutting the bigger pieces. The 6" triangle is convenient for the smaller pieces.

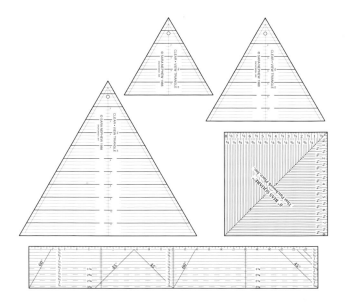

Equilateral-Triangle Graph Paper. This graph paper is useful for designing your own blocks. If you have trouble finding it, check the "Resources" on page 102 for ordering information.

16

Sewing Machine. Use a good-quality sewing machine kept in good working order. Keep lint out of the bobbin case and oil your machine regularly.

Check the stitches for balanced tension every time you oil the machine. Too-loose tension causes weak seams. Too-tight tension produces puckered seams. Your sewing machine manual will show you how to recognize correct tension.

Needles. Dull or bent needles can make poor stitches, so replace the needle occasionally even if it isn't broken or doesn't have a burr. Use a size 80/12 needle and set the stitch length to 10 to 12 stitches per inch. Choose a stitch length long enough to allow your seam ripper to fit into the stitches should you need to remove them.

Seam Ripper. This tool is very useful for removing stitches without stressing the seam or distorting the fabric.

Thread. Even if the quilt you are making is not intended to be a family heirloom, the thread you use is important. Choosing 100% cotton thread when you're sewing on cotton fabric may be more critical than you think. Over time, polyester threads can cut the fabric. This happens because the thread is stronger than the fabric. I have seen this happen in less than ten years.

I have even seen the tangled knots at the beginning of a seam wear holes through the fabric. Try to make a habit of holding the ends of the thread when starting to sew to avoid these knots.

CUTTING STRIPS

To cut a strip accurately, you must begin with a cut edge that is perpendicular to the fold of the fabric. First, fold the fabric in half lengthwise, matching selvages. If the fabric wrinkles along the fold, move the top layer of fabric to the right or left to eliminate the wrinkles.

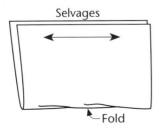

Place the fabric on the mat with the excess fabric to the right and the fold closest to you. (Reverse the direction of the fabric on the mat if you are left-handed.) Place the perpendicular line (center line) of the triangle ruler exactly on the fold, with the base to the left and near the raw edges. Place the ruler against the base of the triangle. Be sure the long cutting guide lies fully on the mat.

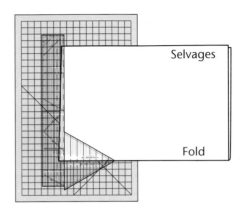

Remove the triangle ruler and, pushing the cutter away from you, make one long cut along the ruler's edge, cleaning and straightening the edges of the fabric.

Fold the fabric in half again, matching the just-cut edges. A shorter cut makes the ruler easier to control. The fabric is now in position to cut strips the required width.

Center the line of the ruler with the correct measurement over the cut edge of the fabric. Cut along the edge of the ruler as shown.

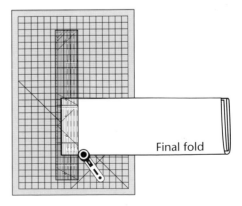

When cutting strips from fabric, open a strip to check for "the bends" after each 18" of fabric you cut. Crooked strips occur when the ruler does not line up exactly perpendicular to the fold.

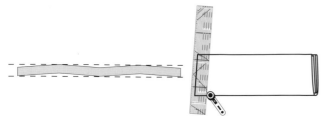

If necessary, open up one fold of the remaining fabric and straighten the edge again before continuing to cut.

FIGURING STRIP WIDTH

In 60° triangle patchwork, the size of the triangle is determined by measuring the height of the triangle rather than the length of its side.

The triangle in the illustration below has a 6" perpendicular measurement or height, so it is called a 6" triangle. The height is perpendicular to the triangle's base.

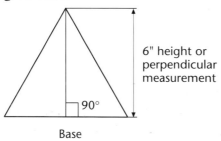

I graphed all of the designs included in this book on equilateral-triangle graph paper. The *finished* measurement of each piece is determined by the scale set for each triangle on the graph paper. In the example below, the scale is one triangle equals 1". Count the number of rows of triangles in the piece and multiply by the scale. Always add the seam allowance last.

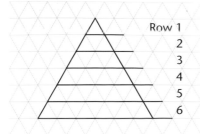

The patterns in this book use a scale of either 1½" or 2". Enlarge or reduce the patterns according to your design needs. If you consider the triangle in the previous illustration as a pieced block, a scale of 1½" will produce 9" finished blocks (6 x 1½" = 9"), and a scale of 2" produces 12" finished blocks (6 x 2" = 12").

The basic rule to determine the strip width is to find the measurement of the finished height of the desired piece and add the width of the seam allowance. Read the following section to find the amount to add for the seam allowance.

CUTTING PIECES

After the strip is cut, open the last fold of the strip and cut pieces from two layers at a time. Always begin cutting at the selvage end of the strip. If necessary, open the strip at the remaining (first) fold and cut one more piece. For even quicker cutting, layer two strips, matching edges exactly. The rotary cutter can easily handle four layers.

Equilateral Triangles

For a drafted equilateral triangle, if you add a ¼" seam allowance to each side, you will see that you actually added ¾" to the triangle's perpendicular measurement, so cut a strip ¾" wider than the triangle's finished height.

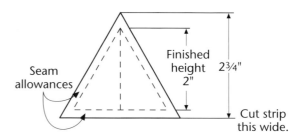

Once the strip is cut, place the triangle ruler on the strip, with the left edge of the ruler to one side of the selvage ends. Match the ruled line for the correct-size triangle with the lower edge of the strip. Place the point of the ruler on the upper edge of the strip as shown. Cut on each side of the triangle ruler.

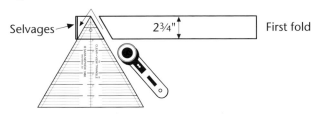

For successive cuts, slide the triangle over only until the side of the ruler comes to the point of the last triangle. Cut on both sides of the triangle ruler again and continue across the strip. There is no need to flip the ruler.

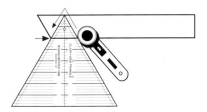

Some quilters don't feel comfortable with the accuracy of the triangles cut from the upper part of the strip. Other quilters find it awkward to cut on both sides of the triangle. An alternate method is to reposition the triangle ruler for each cut, always cutting on the right side of the triangle ruler. For the first cut, position the ruler right side up on its base, then, for the second cut, tip it and place its ruled line on the angled cut as shown.

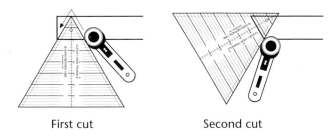

First cut   Second cut

If you are right-handed, begin cutting from the left end of the strip; if you are left-handed, begin from the right end of the strip.

Sandwich-Pieced Equilateral Triangles

Quite often, where there is one equilateral triangle, there will be another triangle sewn next to it. Pre-sewing or sandwich piecing these units is easier and more accurate than handling the triangles individually.

To sandwich-piece, cut two contrasting strips of fabric the same width as for individual triangles. With right sides together, sew ¼"-wide seams along *both* edges of the strips. (See "Sewing Accurate Seam Allowances" on page 25 before beginning.) Press the strips together just as they come off the sewing machine to straighten them.

Cut the triangles as you did for single triangles, matching the ruled line for the correct triangle size. Remove the few stitches at the tip—they will come out easily—then press the seam allowances to one side toward the dark fabric.

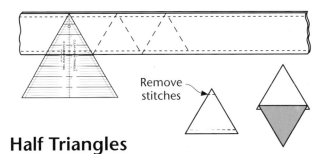

Remove stitches

Half Triangles

The half triangle is one of two shapes that has a mirror image, though not all designs use both images. Use half triangles at the edges of a quilt to square it up. These are often larger in comparison to the other pieces cut for the design, but they are still in scale when sewn.

If the design uses the half triangle and its mirror image, cut triangles 1¼" larger than the finished measurement and then bisect them. For example, for two mirror-image half triangles with a finished perpendicular measurement of 2", cut a triangle with a height of 3¼" and cut it in half.

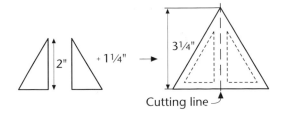

Cutting line

To bisect a triangle, match the perpendicular line of the triangle ruler to an edge of the triangle and cut it in half.

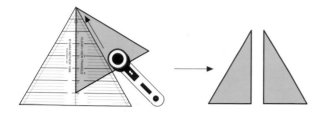

Half triangles can also be cut from rectangles. The patterns use rectangles when it is a more efficient use of the fabric or when only *identical* half triangles are needed.

To cut half triangles from rectangles, cut a strip equal to the width of the base of the *cut* half triangle (including the 1¼" extra). For a half triangle that finishes 4" tall, measure half the base of a 5¼" triangle. Cut the strip 3" wide, cut rectangles 5¼" long, then cut the half triangles.

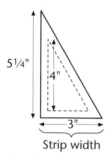

Strip width

For accuracy, place the perpendicular line of the ruler on the long edge of the rectangle, with the point of the ruler on the edge of the fabric. Cut the half triangle. Reverse the remainder of the rectangle and check the opposite half triangle for accuracy.

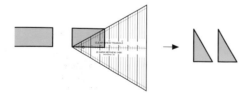

Cut half triangles from a single thickness of fabric unless directed otherwise. Cutting two rectangles with the wrong sides together results in half triangles and their mirror images.

Diamonds

To determine the strip width for cutting diamonds, add a ¼"-wide seam allowance to the diamond's finished measurements. This will add 1" to its height. Divide this measurement in half and cut the strip to this measurement. For example, a 4" finished diamond equals a 5" cut diamond. Cut the strip width half of 5", or 2½" wide. You may see this more easily if you count the number of rows between parallel sides of the diamond, multiply by the scale, and add ½" to allow for ¼"-wide seams.

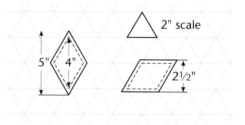

2" scale

To cut diamonds, tip the top of the triangle ruler to the left and use its lower edge to measure and cut a diamond the same length as the width of the strip. Cut the first diamond, allowing extra for cutting off the selvage end. Rotate and trim the piece to the correct size.

For successive cuts, measure with the ruled lines and place the ¼" line

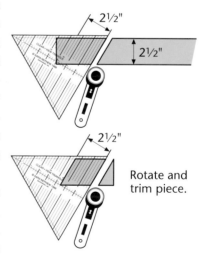

Rotate and trim piece.

along the edge of the triangle ruler on the top edge of the fabric. This way, it is easier to see the fabric edge and does not affect the measurements of the piece being cut. It also ensures accurate cuts.

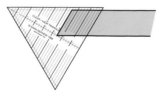

Double Diamonds

The designs in this book frequently use double diamonds. Piece these shapes quickly and accurately by using strip-piecing techniques.

Sew contrasting strips of fabric into the necessary sequence for the design. With the strips still right sides together, press, then open out and press with right sides up to avoid tucks along the seam. Be sure to press the strips straight and flat.

To avoid tucks along the fold, press with right sides up. Begin each stroke with the iron on the light strip and glide it across to the dark strip.

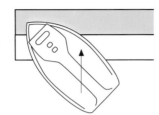

Layer the strip sets, offsetting them ¼" to allow for the thickness of the seam allowances.

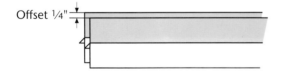

Offset ¼"

Begin cutting as you do for diamonds, using the lower edge of the triangle. Take a generous cut for the first piece and rotate it to clean up the selvage.

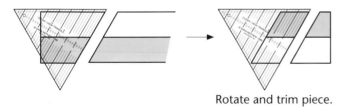

Rotate and trim piece.

Cut each strip into double-diamond units the same width as an individual diamond (the width of each cut strip in the strip-pieced unit).

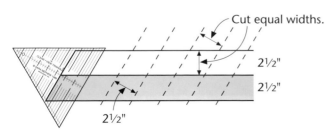

Cut equal widths.

2½"

2½"

2½"

For a diamond four-patch unit, sew two double-diamond units together. Be sure to sew them in the correct order for your design, as it is easy to reverse them.

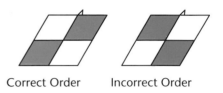

Correct Order Incorrect Order

Three-Patch Triangles

This three-patch triangle unit is found in several of the designs in the pattern section.

The traditional way of piecing this unit is to add a triangle to two adjacent sides of the diamond. Like many of the common units in traditional patchwork blocks, you can piece this unit more accurately if the sewing is done before cutting the unit.

Begin by making *uneven* diamond four-patch units. Cut the strip for the diamond, following the directions on page 20, or refer to your pattern for the required strip width. Cut the triangle strips 1¼" wider than the finished triangle size.

For example, cutting a three-patch triangle unit using a 2" scale requires a 2½"-wide strip for the diamond and a 3¼"-wide strip for the triangles.

Sew the strips together. Crosscut into segments the same width as the strip that you cut for the diamonds.

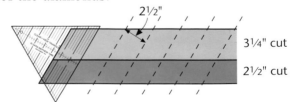

2½"

3¼" cut

2½" cut

Sew the uneven diamond four-patch units together as shown on page 22. The seams do not meet in the center, but each seam begins and ends with a triangle tip. (See "Joining Triangle Patchwork" on pages 26–27.) Turn the piece over and clip the seam allowance halfway down the seam. Press each end of the seam allowance toward the dark fabric.

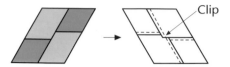

Place the triangle ruler on the four-patch unit, aligning the ¼" line of the triangle ruler at the inner point of the diamond. Measure and cut (4¾" in the example) the first three-patch triangle. Turn the remaining piece, measure, and trim the second three-patch triangle. A tip of each unit will be missing, but the seam allowance will be adequate so it won't pose a problem.

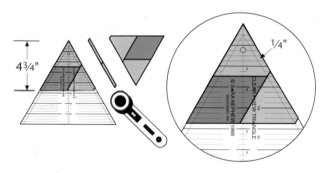

Loose Half Diamonds

Drafting a half diamond and adding ¼"-wide seam allowances adds 1⅞" to its overall height. First, calculate the half diamond's cut height, then measure the width to find the strip width (or refer to your pattern for the required strip width). Unfortunately, there is no clear formula for figuring the strip width for half diamonds.

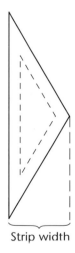

Strip width

To cut loose half diamonds, place the strip vertically on the cutting mat. With the ruler's point toward you, match the perpendicular line of the triangle to the left edge of the strip and match the

point of the triangle to the selvage edge of the strip. Cut off the selvage end.

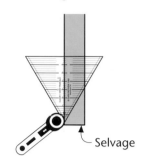

Selvage

Turn the triangle ruler around and match the perpendicular line of the triangle ruler to the left edge of the fabric again. Make sure the ruler intersects the right edge of the strip at the point and cut a half diamond 1⅞" longer than the finished length.

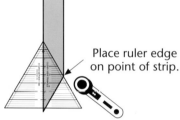

Place ruler edge on point of strip.

For the remainder of the cuts, keep the triangle ruler right side up but alternate the placement of the ruler's perpendicular line to the right and left edge of the strip. Alternate each cut to the left and right edges of the ruler.

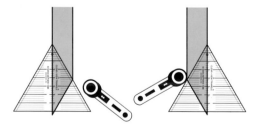

Another method is to flip the strip over after each cut so that you always cut off the right side of the triangle.

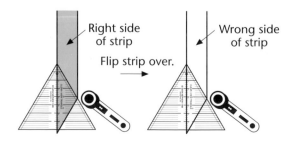

Right side of strip

Flip strip over.

Wrong side of strip

Strip-Pieced Half Diamonds

Use a strip-piecing method to quickly piece these pairs of half diamonds. Not only is it easier to press bigger strips than little pieces, but the strips do not become distorted when pressed.

For this method, cut the strips as directed in the pattern. Sew a pair of contrasting strips together with a ¼"-wide seam allowance. Press the seam allowances toward the darker strip. Sew the pairs of strips together to make a strip-pieced panel.

Find the desired diamond size on the perpendicular line of the ruler and place this point on the edge of the panel with the seam under the ruler's perpendicular line. Cut on each side of the triangle ruler. I found the small rotary cutter helpful for this step.

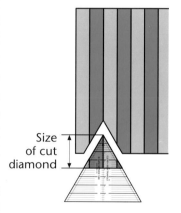

Size of cut diamond

Turn the piece around and match the seam with the ruler's perpendicular line, and the diamond's point with the desired measurement. Cut again, trimming the excess.

Continue cutting one diamond at a time from the strip-pieced panel in the order shown. You may cut all of the diamonds from the panel before turning them around for trimming.

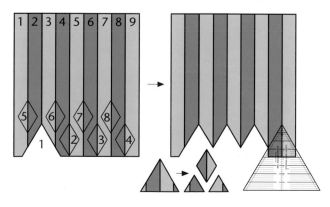

Parallelograms

Parallelograms are similar to diamonds except that parallelograms are longer. Figure the strip width for parallelograms by adding ½" to the finished height to allow for ¼"-wide seam allowances. For example, a 2" parallelogram requires a 2½"-wide strip.

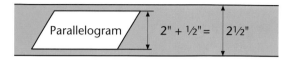

Parallelogram   2" + ½" =   2½"

A graphed parallelogram will show that it is two or three times the length of a diamond or longer, but always in scale. The length is determined by multiplying the number of rows of triangles in the graph paper times the scale plus ½" for seam allowances. Drawn two rows long on the graph, the parallelogram in our example would be cut 4½" long.

Begin cutting parallelograms as you do for diamonds, cutting against the lower edge of the triangle ruler. Take a generous first cut so that you can remove the selvage when the piece is rotated.

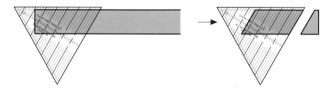

After cutting off the first piece, match a ruled line and the ¼" line along the edge of the triangle with the strip, as shown, to ensure accuracy.

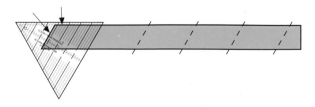

If a design calls for half of the parallelograms to be cut in reverse to produce mirror images, leave your strip folded as you cut. If you want all the parallelograms cut at the same angle, unfold the strip before cutting. If cutting a parallelogram off the left side of the strip results in the wrong angle, then turn the fabric strip over.

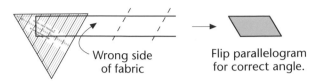

Wrong side of fabric

Flip parallelogram for correct angle.

Trapezoids

Don't let the word scare you. Trapezoids are also easy to cut. Calculate the strip width you cut for trapezoids the same way you do for parallelograms, cutting strips ½" wider than the finished height to allow for ¼"-wide seams.

Notice that a trapezoid is the base of a larger imaginary triangle. Use the formula given on page 18 to calculate the size of that triangle (add ¾" to the height of the triangle). Match the lower edge of the fabric with the ruler's mark representing the base of the imaginary cut triangle. Cut on both sides of the triangle ruler as shown.

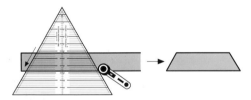

For the next piece, rotate the triangle ruler. Position it to align the mark representing the base of the imaginary cut triangle with the upper edge of the fabric strip. Cut on the right side of the ruler as shown. In this example, the strip width is 2½", and the height of the imaginary triangle is 8¾".

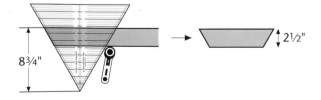

If trapezoids are cut taller than your triangle ruler, use a combination of rulers butted up against each other to arrive at the proper size and angle.

For example, if you need to cut 9¾"-tall trapezoids from a 2" strip and you are using an 8"

ruler, first cut a 60° angle off one end of the strip. Place the triangle ruler 1¾" (9¾" - 8" = 1¾") from the lower edge of the strip. Butt a straight edge against it as shown. Remove the triangle and cut against the straight edge.

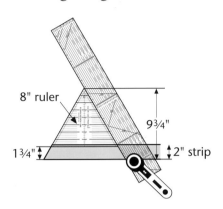

8" ruler

9¾"

1¾"

2" strip

Hexagons and Gemstones

As you did for parallelograms and trapezoids, add ½" to the finished height of the hexagon to determine the width to cut a strip. First, cut diamonds from the strip, then cut off an equilateral triangle from each end of the diamond. (For gemstones, cut a triangle off one end.)

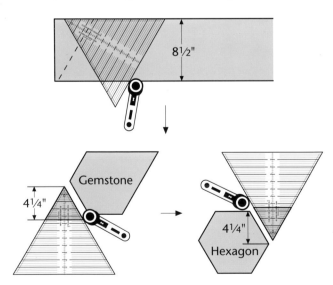

8½"

Gemstone

4¼"

4¼"

Hexagon

Calculate the size of the triangle to cut off by dividing the strip width in half. In the example above, to cut hexagons from a strip 8½" wide, first cut off 8½" diamonds. Then cut a 4¼" equilateral triangle from each point. These triangles won't be in scale with the rest of your project, but you can cut them down to 2¾" triangles.

SEWING TRIANGLE PATCHWORK

SEWING ACCURATE SEAM ALLOWANCES: THE SECRET TO SUCCESS

The last step you must do before beginning to sew is to test your seam allowance. Learning to sew an accurate seam allowance is one of the most important skills quilters can learn. Using an accurate seam allowance will prevent complications throughout the course of the project.

Most of us assume that everyone's ¼"-wide seam allowance measures the same. This would be true if we all used the same rulers and used them identically. The fact is, not all rulers measure the same. Some of us measure to the right or left side of the line on the ruler rather than exactly on the line, which can affect the measurements. Complicate this with presser feet of varying widths and the ways in which we align the fabric under the feet. It is no wonder quilters' seams don't measure the same.

It is better to take this simple test now to determine if your seam allowance is the proper width than to have to fudge things later. Do take this test even if you have a ¼" foot, so you will know how to line up the fabric under the foot. Even if the difference is one thread or two, or if no fabric at all is showing at the edge of the foot, it does make a difference!

Cut a strip of fabric 1½" wide. Cut off three pieces, each 5" long. Sew them together along their long edges with your usual ¼"-wide seam allowance. Press and measure the width of each strip. The finished width of the sewn three-strip

unit should now equal *exactly* 3½". If it does not, repeat the test, adjusting the seam allowance by taking a slightly wider or narrower seam until you find the correct width.

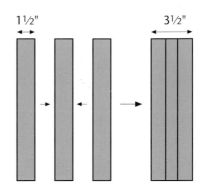

When you find the proper place to position your fabric, mark the throat plate with one or more layers of masking tape. Even if your foot is an accurate ¼" or you can adjust the needle, you will find that the tape relieves eye strain as you feed the fabric against the edge of the layered tape.

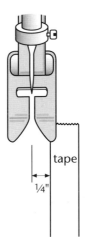

Repeat the test with the tape in place to be sure it is positioned accurately. This is an important step because machines don't always feed straight. (Ask your sewing-machine repair person to adjust this.) In addition, marking the throat plate with a fine-point permanent pen will help you position the tape if you need to replace it or remove it for machine quilting.

USING THE SEAM RIPPER

If you need to rip out seams, it is important to know the correct way to use a seam ripper. I cringe whenever I see a student in one of my classes removing the seam by pulling apart the two pieces and cutting the exposed thread between them. This method is unsatisfactory because, without question, it stretches the edges of the fabric.

Incorrect

The proper way to use the seam ripper is to cut the top thread approximately every five stitches along the length of the seam.

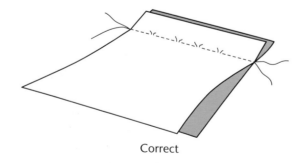

Correct

Flip the work over and pull off the bobbin thread. The two pieces separate as if they'd never been sewn.

I remember the directions that came with the first seam ripper I had for home economics class in seventh grade. The directions said to cut the thread every six *inches*. Obviously, this didn't work. I thought it meant every six *stitches*, but instead, I ripped seams the "wrong" way. That was fine for garment sewing. I wasn't a quilter long when I realized that I was stretching pieces and causing myself a lot of grief.

JOINING TRIANGLE PATCHWORK

Sewing 60° patchwork isn't any more difficult than any other straight-line sewing. Only one of the designs in this book brings more than six seams together at one point. As you sew, you will become familiar with how to line up pieces for sewing.

Nearly every seam will have at least one piece with a 60° angle. Whenever possible, begin sewing at this 60° corner. When the pieces are lined up correctly, they will form ¼" triangle extensions, often called "mouse ears." In the beginning, you may find it helpful to hold the pair of pieces you are sewing up to the ¼" triangle extension shown on page 28. Do not trim the little triangle extensions. They make great notches for matching up seams.

In 60° triangle patchwork, each piece naturally has at least two bias edges. Bias edges are easy to handle if you know how. Any time you are working with bias, exercise care so the fabric doesn't stretch. This means no pushing or pulling to smooth out the block. A general rule in any patchwork is to sew a straight-of-grain edge (threads running parallel to the selvage) to a bias edge (imaginary line drawn at a 45° angle to the selvage) to help stabilize the bias and to keep your blocks lying flat.

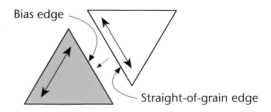

Bias edge
Straight-of-grain edge

As you sew the smaller units, just finger-press the seam before crossing it with other seams. As the units become larger or more complex, use the iron. Gently let the heat of the iron set the seams in the direction you want, and your block will lie smooth. Glide the iron gently in the direction of the grain to help prevent stretched bias edges. A light touch with the iron is easy if you use a light-weight iron. My favorite in my sewing room is a travel iron.

As you join units or blocks, use pins to align seams and hold them in place. You'll find that if a bias edge has stretched a little, you can easily ease it into place.

I have often read to place the piece with the bias edge that must be eased on the bottom so the feed dogs take up the slack. I have never had any luck doing it this way. I either get tucks or end up with one piece longer than it should be. Often, a quick little tug on the end of the pieces can take up the slack once the seam has been started.

Try sewing with the longer bias edge on top and coax the extra fullness into the seam by pushing the stretched bias edge toward the needle with your seam ripper.

Use seam ripper to gently and lightly guide upper fabric layer toward the needle while stitching.

It's important to remember to always ease the piece that has stretched. Steam pressing helps to shrink it back to the proper size after you have sewn all sides.

Chain Piecing

Chain-piece paired-up pieces by feeding each pair into the machine without stopping to lift the presser foot or clip threads. Use this technique whenever possible for the most efficient use of your time and thread.

To chain-piece, spread out the block pieces, following the block diagram, and stack identical pieces together. Pick up two pieces to be sewn together, placing them right sides together and making sure they are correctly positioned. Set them aside and line up the next two pieces. Place them on top of the first pair, offsetting them slightly so that later, after all the pieces are paired, it will be easy to pick them up.

Stack each pair in approximately the same position so that when sewing them, you always feed the same edge with the same piece on top into the machine. For a large quantity, stack them onto several sheets of cardboard.

When you have paired up all the pieces, begin sewing them. Check at first to be sure you are sewing the correct edge. Resist the temptation to open every pair before sewing them. As long as the previous seam was sewn correctly, use it as a guide for feeding the next pair of pieces. Don't lift the presser foot between seams, just continue to sew one pair after another.

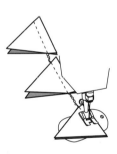

Chain piecing

The pieces will be "chained" together with twisted threads between the pairs. In addition to the advantages of saving time and thread, there won't be lots of thread ends to trim.

I like to keep the chain together when I take it to the ironing board and cut the threads after pressing. Press, clip, and stack, and you're ready for the next step without having to reorganize.

You can also chain-piece blocks the way you chain small pieces. After you have pieced the blocks, join them into rows. I find it easiest to first join the blocks by pairs into diamonds. Look at the quilt plan and count the number of pairs of triangle blocks that are repeated in the whole quilt. Sew these together.

Sew these diamond-shaped blocks into rows. As you join the diamond blocks, the seam will cross the previously sewn seam. Finger-press the end of the seam in the desired direction as you sew, pressing them in the direction of least resistance, then press the seams between the blocks after the row is complete. Join rows.

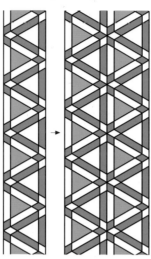

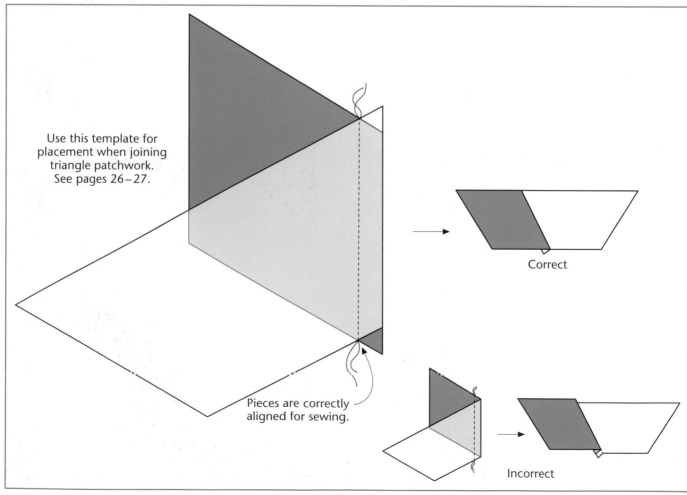

Use this template for placement when joining triangle patchwork. See pages 26–27.

Pieces are correctly aligned for sewing.

Correct

Incorrect

◄ Star Flurries

**Wall Hanging
by Gayle Bong, 1994,
Elkhorn, Wisconsin,
36" x 41".**
This wall hanging is a
smaller version of the
Star Flurries quilt below.

Star Flurries ▶

**by Gayle Bong, 1994,
Elkhorn, Wisconsin,
80½" x 88".**
Six-pointed stars
are traditionally done
using all diamonds and
set-in piecing. Triangle
blocks eliminate the
need for set-ins. This
variation uses the
folded-corner
technique. The colors
were inspired by an
antique quilt in
my collection.
Directions begin
on page 79.

Smoothing Iron ▲

**by Lorry Taylor, 1994,
Mukwonago, Wisconsin,
51" x 54".**
For this variation of Echo Point,
Lorry used the pretty floral
fabric in the stars as the basis
for selecting the other fabrics.
The pattern is a good candidate
for using scraps.

Hot Stuff

◄

**by Gayle Bong, 1994,
Elkhorn, Wisconsin,
51" x 54".**
This old pattern combines one
easy block in two colorations.
In this variation of Echo Point,
fabrics were placed in a
positive/negative arrangement.

Echo Point ▶

**by Gayle Bong, 1994,
Elkhorn, Wisconsin,
51" x 54".**
This design was inspired
by the Smoothing Iron pattern.
I remembered the block, but
not how the alternating blocks
were colored. This version
creates an illusion of
transparency. Choose the
border fabric first to make
fabric selection easier.
Directions begin on page 42.

Fall Festival

**by Gayle Bong, 1994,
Elkhorn, Wisconsin,
53½" x 61".**
This quilt was made while
anticipating the glorious colors
of falling autumn leaves. With
the blocks set to create
the illusion of leaves floating
to the ground, one almost
expects to see a pile of them
at the bottom of the quilt.
Directions begin on page 47.

Autumn's Twilight ▶

**by Pat Titus, 1994,
Burlington, Wisconsin,
56" x 61".**
The enthusiasm Pat has for
autumn shows in her choices of
fabric for the abstract leaves in
this Fall Festival variation.

◄ Little Luvs

**by Gayle Bong, 1994,
Elkhorn, Wisconsin,
25" x 26½".**
This quilt, made of the small hearts from Lots of Luvs, makes a wonderful companion piece to the large quilt, or a darling quilt to hang anywhere you want to spread a little love.
Directions begin on page 51.

Lots of Luvs ►

**by Gayle Bong, 1990,
Elkhorn, Wisconsin,
53½" x 74½".**
Two Heart blocks combine to create this warm and loving quilt. Strip piecing the small pieces simplifies the job.
Directions begin on page 54.

Cosmic Columbines ▶

**by Gayle Bong, 1994,
Elkhorn, Wisconsin,
54" x 59".**
Blue columbines in space?
That's the illusion created by
the two blocks in this quilt,
where cloudlike fabric in the
background enhances the
effect of the columbines on
the trellis. Directions begin
on page 84.

◀ ## Sunday Best

**by Gayle Bong, 1993,
Elkhorn, Wisconsin,
50" x 53".**
The striking simplicity of
a two-color quilt is enhanced by
the feathered heart quilted in
the alternate plain blocks.
Quilted by Jeanne Bliss.

Triplicity ▶

**by Rose Lauchart, 1994,
Mukwonago, Wisconsin,
85" x 109".**
This quilt consists of two
triangle blocks that use the
three-patch triangle units. The
large empty spaces are the
perfect place to showcase your
quilting skills. The pieced
border makes this a
special quilt. Directions
begin on page 61.

◀ # Triplicity

**by Valerie Bonhivert, 1994,
Antioch, Illinois,
68½" x 76½".**
The sunny yellow stars
in the background of Valerie's
quilt contribute to the glowing
effect. The three-patch triangle
technique makes this
a quick project. Directions
begin on page 61.

35

Dancing Diamonds

**by Gayle Bong, 1994,
Elkhorn, Wisconsin,
87" x 88".**
This is another easy
two-block design using quick
cutting and piecing. Either
block alone creates a pattern
of interlocking diamond rings.
When combined, the two
rings overlap, creating
movement and depth.
Quilted by Peg Ries.

Thousand Pyramids ▶

**by Mary Novak,1991,
Mukwonago, Wisconsin,
36" x 48".**
Thousand Pyramids was the
most common design in my
search for quilts with repeating
triangle blocks. Mary's variation
alternates units of four light
triangles with units of four dark
triangles in offset rows, creating
a zigzag effect. Although the
light and dark triangles aren't
always grouped together, other
arrangements of these simple
triangle blocks are possible.

◄ Potluck

**by Linda Bohling, 1994,
Mukwonago, Wisconsin,
74½" x 76½".**
Linda created an antique scrap
look in her quilt by selecting
reproduction prints. Setting the
block with an alternate plain
block also contributed to
its antique look. Directions
begin on page 58.

Stacked Pyramids ►

**by Gayle Bong, 1994,
Elkhorn, Wisconsin,
60" x 76".**
This was one of the first
triangle quilts I made, inspired
by an antique quilt simply
known as Triangles, shown in
the book *Pieces of the Past*
by Nancy J. Martin .
(That Patchwork Place).

Trio of Triangles ▶

**by Gayle Bong, 1994,
Elkhorn, Wisconsin,
69½" x 73½".**
Using the three-patch triangle technique makes it fast and easy to create this illusion of overlapping triangles. Select fabrics carefully to make the triangles stand out. Directions begin on page 70.

◀ Trio of Triangles

**by Gayle Bong, 1994,
Elkhorn, Wisconsin,
69½" x 73½".**
I intended to use the same light fabric in the center of each triangle. Adding the yellow was an afterthought, which added a spark to this masculine quilt. Quilted by Carrie Stanek and Nancy Linz.

▲ Trio of Triangles

by Sally Parker, 1994,
Mundelein, Illinois,
66" x 70".
Constructing the three-patch
triangle unit in three different
colorations makes this design go
together in a snap.

Magic Jewels

**by Gayle Bong, 1994,
Elkhorn, Wisconsin,
42½" x 49½".**
When joined side by
side, the light stars in each
of the two blocks recede to
become background, and a
folded star appears.
Directions begin
on page 75.

Desert Ice ▶

**by Gayle Bong, 1994,
Elkhorn, Wisconsin,
30½" x 35½".**
Half diamonds merge
on the sides of the blocks,
creating arrows, which when
shaded from light to dark,
appear to be darting.
Repeating the arrows at
the edge provides an
effective border for this
hexagonal wall quilt.
Directions begin
on page 90.

USING THE PATTERNS

The pattern section includes complete directions for rotary cutting and constructing eleven quilts, which are presented from the easiest to most challenging. Before beginning, read through the pattern for an understanding of how the quilt will be constructed. Make your fabric selections and construct a sample block to assure yourself that you are pleased with your choices and that you understand how to cut and sew the pieces. Finished block size refers to the height of the triangle forming the block, without the seam allowances. All cutting directions include a ¼"-wide seam allowance.

Some plans require that you cut two different shapes from the same-width strip, so carefully count the pieces as you cut them. A leftover 30"-long strip is more useful than ten extra diamonds.

Yardage is based on 42" of usable width. This allows for shrinkage and removal of selvages from 44"-wide fabric. Some fabrics are slightly wider and you may be able to cut an extra piece from those strips. Occasionally, you may need to cut one or two extra pieces from the remaining fabric or from scraps without having to cut an entire strip. Fabric requirements allow for this. If the number of pieces is omitted from the cutting chart, then additional cutting directions follow, or the strips are used for strip piecing.

The patterns refer to the colors shown in the color photographs of the quilts. Feel free to choose fabrics in colors you enjoy. You may want to use colors from the same side of the color wheel as directed. For example, if the pattern calls for blue, which is a cool color, substitute green or purple.

Likewise, substitute a different warm color (pink, gold, red, orange) if desired. Use the diagram provided with each pattern to experiment with color.

The patterns specify how much fabric is needed for the quilt backing and also indicates how to orient the backing seam. Cut the backing yardage in half across the width of the fabric, then join the long edges together. Be sure to cut backings an extra 4" to 5" larger than the quilt top to allow 2" to 2½" on each side.

You may center the seam on the quilt backing, or for a more economical use of fabric, place the seam to one side. The smaller quilts are good candidates for combining leftovers from the front for an interesting "pieced" backing. Be sure to measure and cut binding strips before piecing the backing with leftovers.

Each cutting chart specifies the number and shape of pieces to cut. Use the following key as a guide.

KEY

Name	Shape
Triangle	△
Diamond	▱
Half Diamond	◁
Rectangle	▭
Trapezoid	⏢
Hexagon	⬡

echo point

COLOR PHOTO
ON PAGE
31

QUILT SIZE
Lap 51" x 54"
Queen 78½" x 93"

FINISHED BLOCK SIZE
Lap 9"
Queen 12"

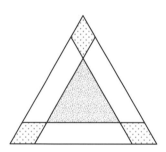

Block A

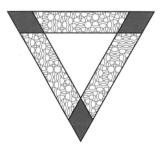

Block B

Lap

Queen

MATERIALS
44"- wide fabric

	LAP	QUEEN
Leaf print	1½ yds.	4½ yds.
Black	½ yd.	¾ yd.
Cream	1⅛ yds.	3¼ yds.
Rust	½ yd.	¾ yd.
Green	½ yd.	1⅛ yds.
Binding	½ yd.	¾ yd.
Backing	3¼ yds.	5¾ yds.

CUTTING

Cut the following strips across the width of the fabric from selvage to selvage, then crosscut into the shapes indicated. Refer to "60°-Angle Rotary Cutting," beginning on page 16.

LAP

Note: For borders, cut 5 strips, each 5" wide, from the leaf print.

Fabric	Strip Width	No. of Strips	No. of Pieces	Shape
Leaf print	2"	11	66*	 trapezoid
Black	2"	4	66	 parallelogram
Cream	2"	12	69*	 trapezoid
	5¼"	2	22	triangle
Rust	2"	5	69	 parallelogram
Green	5¼"	2	23	triangle
Binding	2½"	6	—	—

*Cut trapezoids with lower edge of strip on the ruler's 6¾" mark. (See "Trapezoids" on page 24.)

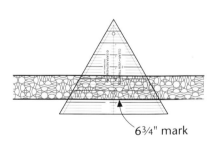

6¾" mark

43

QUEEN

Note: For borders, cut 9 strips, each 5" wide, from the leaf print.

Fabric	Strip Width	No. of Strips	No. of Pieces	Shape
Leaf print	2½"	29	114**	▱
Black	2½"	9	114	▱
Cream	2½"	30	117**	▱
	6¾"	5	38	△
Rust	2½"	9	117	▱
Green	6¾"	5	39	△
Binding	2½"	9	—	—

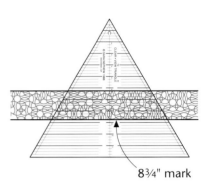

8¾" mark

**Cut trapezoids with lower edge of strip on the ruler's 8¾" mark. (See "Trapezoids" on page 24.)

ASSEMBLING THE BLOCKS

Block A

1. Sew a cream trapezoid to a green triangle. Sew a rust diamond to another cream trapezoid; sew to the triangle unit.

2. Sew a rust diamond to each end of a cream trapezoid. Sew the trapezoid unit to the triangle unit made in step 1 above to complete the block.

Block A
Lap: Make 23 (9" blocks)
Queen: Make 39 (12" blocks)

Block B

1. Sew a leaf print trapezoid to a cream triangle. Sew a black diamond to another leaf print trapezoid; sew to the triangle unit.

2. Sew a black diamond to each end of a leaf print trapezoid. Sew the trapezoid unit to the triangle unit made in step 1 above to complete the block.

Block B
Lap: Make 22 (9" blocks)
Queen: Make 38 (12" blocks)

ASSEMBLING THE QUILT

1. Sew the blocks into horizontal rows. Position each Block A with the green triangle pointing up. Position each Block B with the cream triangle pointing down. Try to position the end blocks so the grain line in the triangles runs parallel with the edges of the quilt.

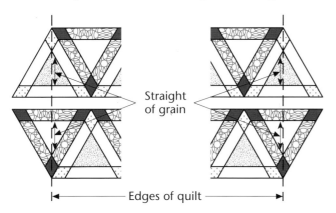

Straight of grain

|← —————— Edges of quilt —————— →|

2. Sew the rows together. The sides of the quilt will zigzag. On the right side of the quilt top, mark the placement line for the border marking ¼" beyond the points of the diamonds to allow for seams.

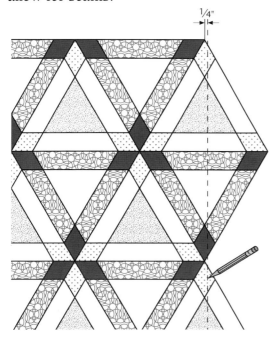

ADDING THE BORDERS

1. Cut the required number of border strips for your quilt size. Sew the strips together end to end as needed. Measure and cut side borders. (See "Adding Borders" on pages 95–97.)

2. Position a long edge of each side border on the marked placement line and sew to the quilt top. Trim the triangle blocks, leaving a ¼"-wide seam allowance. Press seam allowances toward borders.

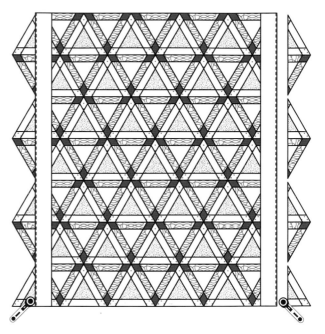

3. Measure, cut, and sew top and bottom borders.

FINISHING UP

1. Mark quilting lines as desired.
2. Layer the quilt top with batting and backing. Orient the backing seam horizontally for the lap size and vertically for the queen size. Baste. (See "Basting" on pages 98–99.)
3. Hand or machine quilt. (See "Quilting" on page 100.)
4. Bind the edges. (See "Binding" on pages 100–101.)

Quilting Suggestion

▲ Quilt ¼" inside the seam line of each leaf print trapezoid and black diamond.

▲ Quilt a group of 3 loops in the cream triangles, and ¼" inside the green triangles.

▲ Choose a commercial quilting stencil to quilt the outside border.

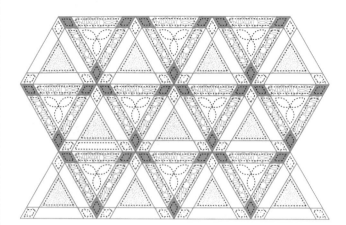

fall festival

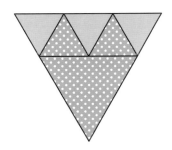

COLOR PHOTO
ON PAGE
32

QUILT SIZE
53½" x 61"

FINISHED BLOCK SIZE
4½"

MATERIALS
44"- wide fabric

20 strips, each 3¾" x 21", of assorted prints for leaflets

20 strips, each 2¼" x 21", of assorted prints for leaflets

¼ yd. brown for stems

2¼ yds. sky blue for background

⅞ yd. for border

½ yd. for binding

3½ yds. for backing

CUTTING

Cut the following strips across the width of the fabric from selvage to selvage, then crosscut into the shapes indicated. Refer to "60°-Angle Rotary Cutting," beginning on page 16. Some of the strips in the chart below have additional cutting requirements. See "Additional Cutting" on page 48. The remaining strips are used for strip piecing.

Fabric	Strip Width	No. of Strips	No. of Pieces	Shape
Brown	2½"	2	—	—
Sky blue	5¼"	3	40*	△
	2¼"	5	140	△
	3⅜"	1	—	—
	2¼"	10	—	—
	5"	2	—	—
	1½"	3	—	—
Border	4½"	6	—	—
Binding	2½"	6	—	—

*Cut one triangle from scraps.

Additional Cutting

Set aside 2½"-wide brown strips for stems. See page 50 for cutting instructions.

Open 3⅜"-wide sky blue strip right side up on mat. Cut 5 rectangles, each 3⅜" x 5¾". Cut diagonally in direction shown for half triangles.

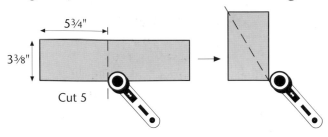

Cut 5

From the 5"-wide sky blue strips, cut 10 rectangles, each 5" x 5⅞". With rectangles right side up, place the perpendicular line of the triangle ruler on the 5" left edge and cut as shown.

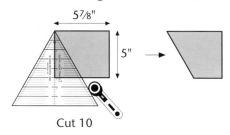

Cut 10

ASSEMBLING THE BLOCKS

1. Cut each of the 10 sky blue 2¼"-wide strips in half crosswise. Sew a blue strip to each of the 2¼" x 21" leaflet print strips, sewing ¼" from each long edge. Cut sandwich-pieced triangles. (See "Sandwich-Pieced Equilateral Triangles" on page 19.)

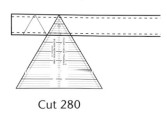

Cut 280

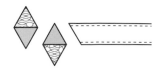

2. Matching leaflet print triangles, sew pairs of sandwich-pieced triangles together and add a 2¼" sky blue triangle to one end.

Make 140

3. From the 3¾" x 21" leaflet print strips, cut a total of 140 triangles.

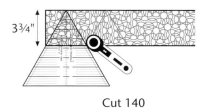

Cut 140

4. Sew a 3¾" large triangle to the unit made in step 2, matching the print of the small triangles. (Mix up a few triangles to make several natural-looking multicolored leaflets.) Press seam toward the large triangle.

Make 140

ASSEMBLING THE QUILT

NOTE

Although this design is based on the block shown below, it will be easier to construct the quilt if you consider each leaflet a block. You will also have more freedom in arranging the colors. If desired, substitute a few leaf units for the sky blue triangles in the rows.

For random placement:

1. Sew 120 of the leaflet blocks together into groups of 3 to make 40 larger units. Sew into rows of 4 units each, separating each unit with a sky blue triangle.

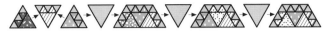

Make 10 rows.

2. Sew 2 leaflet blocks together, then sew a sky blue half triangle to the left end and a sky blue triangle to the right end.

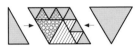

Make 10

3. Sew one of these units to the begining of each row made in step 1. Sew a half trapezoid to the other end of each row. Make all rows identical. Press the seams between the leaves toward the end of the row.

4. Appliqué stems. (See "Stems" on page 50.)

NOTE

Later, when you sew the rows together, rotate every other row 180° so the leaves face each other.

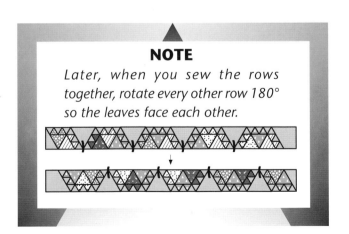

For planned placement:

1. Following the quilt diagram on page 47, arrange the leaves in 10 vertical rows, each consisting of 14 leaflets and 4 sky blue triangles. If desired, group the leaflets according to color or value (light to dark) in a pleasing order.

2. Sew 2 triangle units together to form a diamond. Sew the diamonds together to make a row. Consistently finger-press all the seams in the row in one direction and alternate directions from row to row.

3. Sew a sky blue half trapezoid to the top of every other row and to the bottom of alternate rows. Sew a sky blue half triangle to the remaining end of each row.

4. Applique stems.

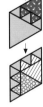
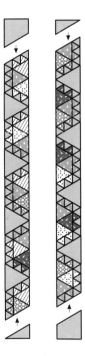

stems

1. Cut 40 bias strips, each 1" wide, from the 2½"-wide brown strips. Place the 45°-angle line of your ruler over the top edge of the fabric strip to cut segments at the correct angle.

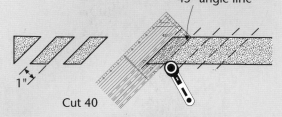

Cut 40

2. Press stems in half, wrong sides together. Stitch ¼" from the fold. Press the seam allowance to the back, trimming if necessary to make sure the raw edges do not show when the strip is turned to the front side.

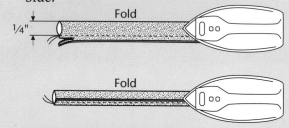

3. Using a blind stitch, appliqué the stem to the large sky blue triangle as shown, extending one end of the stem ½" past the raw edges of the triangle.

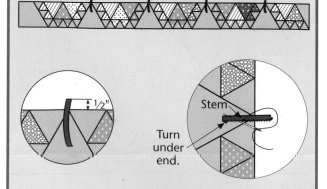

4. Sew the rows together. Press, twisting the seams so the stems lie flat.

ADDING THE BORDERS

1. Join 1½"-wide sky blue background strips end to end. Measure, cut, and sew a sky blue background strip to each side. (See "Using Plain Borders" on page 95.)
2. Join 4½"-wide border strips as needed. Measure, cut, and sew side borders to quilt, then repeat for top and bottom borders.

FINISHING UP

1. Mark quilting lines as desired.
2. Layer the quilt top with batting and backing. Orient the backing seam horizontally. Baste. (See "Basting" on pages 98–99.)
3. Hand or machine quilt. (See "Quilting" on page 100.)
4. Bind the edges. (See "Binding" on pages 100–101.)

Quilting Suggestion

Quilt random wavy lines to represent the wind.

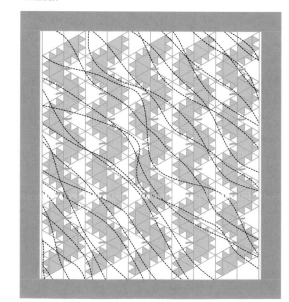

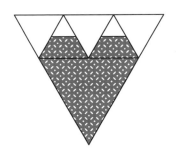

little luvs

COLOR PHOTO
ON PAGE
33

QUILT SIZE
25" x 26½"

FINISHED BLOCK SIZE
4½"

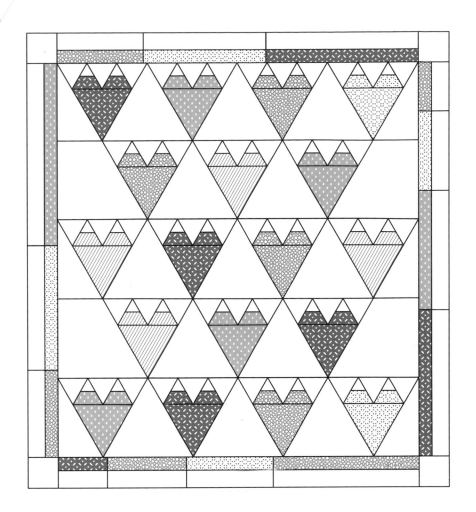

MATERIALS

44"- wide fabric

1¼ yds. tan print for
background and binding

5 squares, each 11" x 11",
assorted dark plaids for
hearts and strip-pieced inner
border

1 yd. backing

CUTTING

Cut the following strips from the tan print background across the width from selvage to selvage, then crosscut into the shapes indicated. Refer to "60°-Angle Rotary Cutting," beginning on page 16. Some of the strips in the chart below have additional cutting requirements. See "Additional Cutting" on page 52. The remaining strips are used for strip piecing.

Note: For binding, cut 3 strips, each 2½" wide.

Strip Width	No. of Strips	No. of Pieces	Shape
5¼"	1	13	△
2¼"	2	54	△
1½"	5	—	—
5¾"	1	—	—
5"	1	—	—

Additional Cutting

From the 5¾"-wide strip, cut 3 triangles, then bisect each triangle to make 6 half triangles.

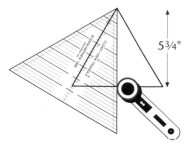

From the 5"-wide strip, cut 2 trapezoids with the lower edge of strip on the ruler's 10¼" mark. Cut trapezoids in half. From scraps, cut 4 squares, each 2¼" x 2¼". (See "Trapezoids" on page 24.)

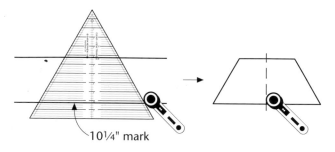

10¼" mark

From each of the dark plaid squares, cut:
1 strip, 3¾" wide. Cut 4 triangles from each of 4 colors; cut 2 triangles from the remaining color for a total of 18 triangles.
4 strips, each 1¼" wide, for strip piecing

ASSEMBLING
THE BLOCKS

1. Sew the 1¼"-wide plaid strips to the 1½"-wide tan strips, placing plaid strips end to end. Press seam toward the dark.

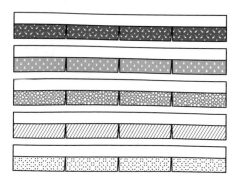

2. Cut 2¼" triangles from the strip sets made in step 1. Use the triangles in which the heart color appears as trapezoids. Each Heart block has 2 of these triangles and one 3¾" matching dark plaid triangle. Count carefully and reserve the remaining strip sets to use for the border. Cut 2 triangles for each 3¾" triangle that you cut.

2½"

Cut 2 for each heart.

Discard these triangles.

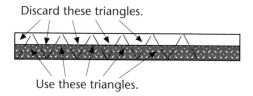

Use these triangles.

3. Sew each strip-pieced triangle to a 2¼" tan triangle.

4. Sew these units together in matching pairs and add a tan triangle to the end as shown. Gently press the trapezoids flat, with seams toward the tan background. Sew the trapezoid unit to a matching 3¾" dark plaid triangle, keeping it on top when you sew, to make sure that the stitching won't cut off the points. Press seam toward the large triangle.

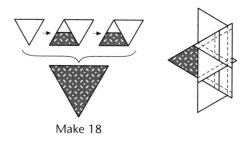

Make 18

ASSEMBLING
THE QUILT

1. Following the quilt diagram, sew the blocks into 3 rows with 4 hearts each, and 2 rows with 3 hearts each. Alternate each Heart block with a 5¼" tan triangle.

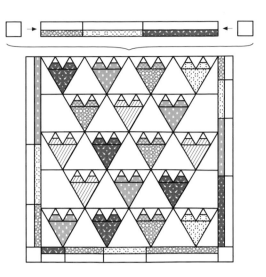

2. Sew a half triangle to each end of a 4-Heart-block row, and a half trapezoid to each end of a 3-Heart-block row. Sew the rows together.

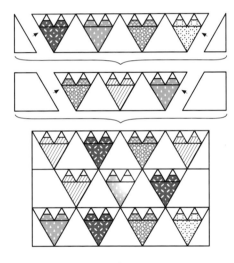

ADDING THE BORDERS

1. Sew the leftover strip sets together, end to end. Measure through the center of the quilt from top to bottom. Cut 2 side border strips to this measurement.
2. Measure through the center of the quilt from side to side. Cut top and bottom borders to this measurement.
3. Sew side borders to the quilt.
4. Sew a 2¼" tan corner square to each end of the top and bottom border. Sew top and bottom borders to the quilt.

FINISHING UP

1. Mark quilting lines as desired.
2. Layer the quilt top with batting and backing. Baste. (See "Basting" on pages 98–99.)
3. Hand or machine quilt. (See "Quilting" on page 100.)
4. Bind the edges. (See "Binding" on pages 100–101.)

Quilting Suggestion

Quilt a heart in each pieced heart and a smaller heart in each alternate plain triangle.

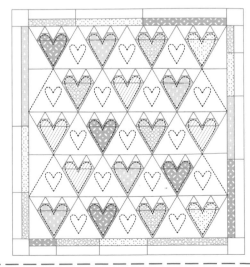

lots of luvs

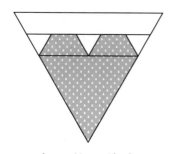

COLOR PHOTO
ON PAGE
33

QUILT SIZE
LAP: 53½" x 74½"
TWIN: 74½" x 92½"

FINISHED BLOCK SIZE
LAP: 9"
TWIN: 9"

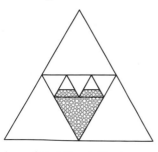

Large Heart Block

Small Heart Block

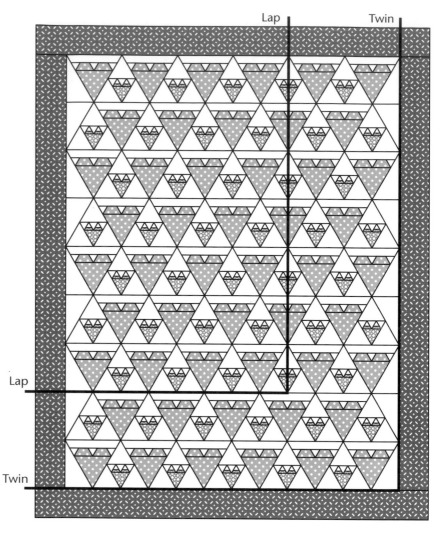

In the directions that follow, this quilt has been simplified by specifying dark red for all of the small Heart blocks. If you wish to make small hearts in more than one fabric, adjust the yardage requirements to include the fabrics of your choice.

MATERIALS
44"- wide fabric

	LAP	TWIN
Light pink for background	2½ yds.	4½ yds.
Medium pink for large hearts	1 yd.	1¾ yds.
Dark red for small hearts	½ yd.	¾ yd.
Border	1⅛ yds.	1½ yds.
Binding	½ yd.	¾ yd.
Backing	3¼ yds.	5½ yds.

CUTTING

Cut the following strips across the width of the fabric from selvage to selvage, then crosscut into the shapes indicated. Refer to "60°-Angle Rotary Cutting," beginning on page 16. The strips without shape designations are used for strip piecing.

LAP

Fabric	Strip Width	No. of Strips	No. of Pieces	Shape
Light pink	2¼"	5	147	△
	2"	7	25*	⏢
	5¼"	7	72	△
	1½"	4	—	—
	6"	2	8**	▭
Med. pink	6¾"	3	25	△
	2"	5	50***	⏢
Dark red	1¼"	4	—	—
	3¾"	2	24	△
Border	6"	6	—	—
Binding	2½"	6	—	—

TWIN

Fabric	Strip Width	No. of Strips	No. of Pieces	Shape
Light pink	2¼"	10	297	△
	2"	13	50*	⏢
	5¼"	14	147	△
	1½"	7	—	—
	6"	3	10**	▭
Med. pink	6¾"	6	50	△
	2"	8	100***	⏢
Dark red	1¼"	7	—	—
	3¾"	3	49	△
Border	6"	8	—	—
Binding	2½"	8	—	—

*Cut light pink trapezoids with the lower edge of strip on the ruler's 9¾" mark. (See "Trapezoids" on page 24.)

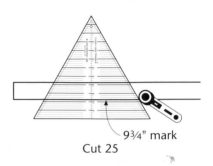

9¾" mark
Cut 25

**Cut rectangles 10¼" long. With pairs of rectangles *wrong* sides together, cut half triangles. You will have 2 half triangles left over to use for another project.

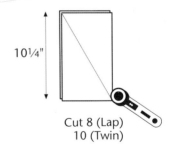

10¼"

Cut 8 (Lap)
10 (Twin)

***Cut medium pink trapezoids with the lower edge of strip on the ruler's 3¾" mark.

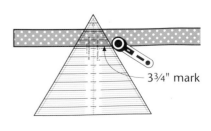

3¾" mark

Cut 50

ASSEMBLING THE BLOCKS

Large Hearts

1. Sew a 2¼" light pink triangle to the right side of each medium pink trapezoid.

Make 50 (Lap)
100 (Twin)

2. Sew these units together in pairs and add a 2¼" light pink triangle to the left end. Gently press the seams toward the trapezoids.

3. Sew the trapezoid unit to one side of a 6¾" medium pink triangle, keeping it on top when you stitch to make sure you don't cut off the points.

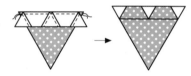

4. Sew a light pink trapezoid to the top to complete the large Heart blocks. Press gently toward the light trapezoid.

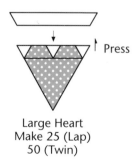

Large Heart
Make 25 (Lap)
50 (Twin)

Small Hearts

1. Sew a 1½"-wide light pink strip to a 1¼"-wide dark red strip. Press seam toward the dark strip.

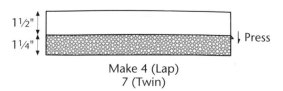

Make 4 (Lap)
7 (Twin)

2. Cut 2¼" triangles from the strip sets made in step 1. Use the triangles in which the heart color appears as trapezoids.

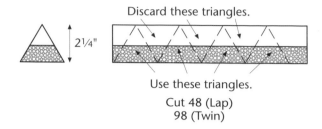

Discard these triangles.

Use these triangles.
Cut 48 (Lap)
98 (Twin)

3. Sew a 2¼" light pink triangle to each of the strip-pieced triangles.

4. Sew the units made in step 3 together in pairs and sew a light pink triangle to the left end. Gently press the trapezoids' seam allowances toward the light pink triangles.

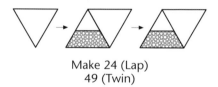

Make 24 (Lap)
49 (Twin)

5. Sew the trapezoid unit to a matching 3¾" dark red triangle, keeping it on top when you sew, to watch for points. Press seam toward the large triangle.

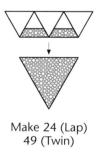

Make 24 (Lap)
49 (Twin)

6. Sew a 5¼" light pink triangle to each side of the little heart, finger-pressing the seam

allowances toward the light triangles after sewing each seam. Press.

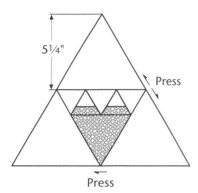

Small Heart
Make 24 (Lap)
49 (Twin)

ASSEMBLING THE QUILT

1. Alternating large and small Heart blocks and following the quilt plan on page 54, arrange into the required number of rows for the quilt size you are making.

   Row 1: Begin and end with a large Heart block.

   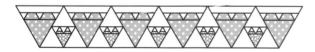

   Row 2: Begin and end with a small Heart block.

   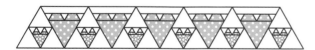

2. Sew a half triangle to both ends of each row. You will have 2 half triangles remaining. Sew the rows together.

   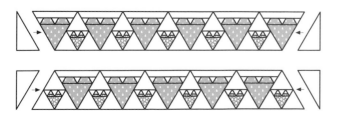

ADDING THE BORDERS

1. Join 6"-wide border strips end to end as needed.
2. Measure, cut, and sew the borders as directed in "Using Plain Borders" on page 95.

FINISHING UP

1. Mark quilting lines as desired.
2. Layer the quilt top with batting and backing. Orient the backing seam horizontally on the lap quilt and vertically on the twin quilt. Baste. (See "Basting" on pages 98–99.)
3. Hand or machine quilt. (See "Quilting" on page 100.)
4. Bind the edges. (See "Binding" on pages 100–101.)

Quilting Suggestion

▲ Quilt a heart in each block.
▲ Use a round template to mark clamshells around the border.

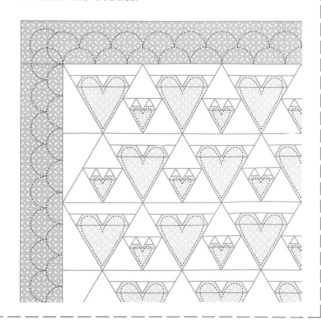

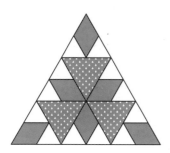

potluck

COLOR PHOTO
ON PAGE
37

QUILT SIZE
74½" x 76½"

FINISHED BLOCK SIZE
12"

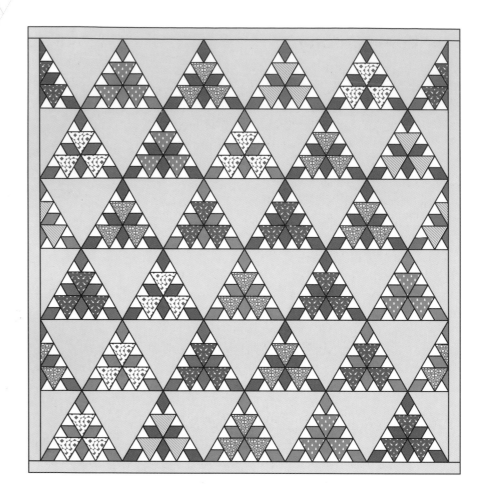

MATERIALS

44"- wide fabric

3⅞ yds. medium light for background setting triangles and border

1¼ yds. total assorted darks

1¼ yds. total assorted mediums

1¼ yds. total assorted lights

⅝ yd. for binding

4½ yds. for backing

CUTTING

Cut the medium light strips across the width of the fabric from selvage to selvage. *Cut all other strips 21" long.* From the strips, crosscut into the shapes indicated. Refer to "60°-Angle Rotary Cutting," beginning on page 16.

Note: For borders, cut 8 strips, each 2½" wide, from the medium light fabric.

Fabric	Strip Width	No. of Strips	No. of Pieces	Shape
Med. light	12¾"	7	27	△
	13¼"	1	3*	△
Darks	2½"	27	162	▱
Mediums	4¾"	14	81	△
Lights	2¾"	27	324	△
Binding	2½"	7	—	—

*Bisect these for half triangles and reverse half triangles at the ends of rows. See "Half Triangles" on pages 19–20.

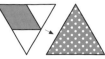

Additional Cutting

For *each* of the 6 half blocks, cut:

1 dark 2½"-wide strip. From this strip, cut 2 diamonds, then trim the strip to 1¹¹/₁₆" and cut 2 half diamonds 5⅞" long. (See "Diamonds" on page 20 and "Loose Half Diamonds" on page 22.)

Cut the following from scraps:

1 medium triangle, 4¾" tall, and 1 half triangle, 5¼" tall* (See "Half Triangles" on pages 19–20.)

6 light triangles, 2¾" tall

*For 3 of the half blocks, cut this half triangle as directed; for the remaining 3 half blocks, cut the half triangles in reverse.

ASSEMBLING
THE BLOCKS

NOTE

In the quilt photo on page 37, all the light, medium, and dark fabrics in each block match, but the fabrics change from block to block. Follow this method, or use many fabrics for a scrappy look, keeping the values the same from block to block.

Full Blocks

1. Sew a light triangle to a dark diamond. Finger-press the seam toward the diamond. Sew a light triangle to the adjacent side of the diamond to make a triangle unit. Press.

Make 6

2. Sew a triangle unit made in step 1 to a medium triangle, to form a diamond-shaped unit.

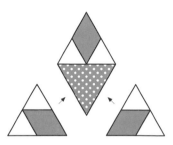

Make 3

3. Sew a triangle unit made in step 1 to 2 adjacent sides of a diamond unit made in step 2.

Make 1

4. Sew a diamond unit to 2 adjacent sides of a triangle unit.

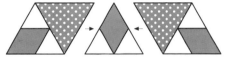

Make 1

5. Join the sections made in steps 3 and 4 to complete the block, pressing seams toward the large triangles.

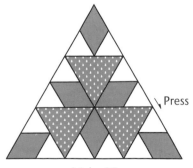

Press

Make 27

Half Blocks and Reverse Half Blocks

1. Repeat step 1 to make 2 triangle units for each half block and reverse half block. Sew a medium triangle to 6 of these units to make diamond units.

Make 6   Make 6

2. For each half block, sew a light triangle to a dark half diamond, forming a half triangle. Make 2 of these units for each half block, then sew 1 of them to a medium half triangle as shown.

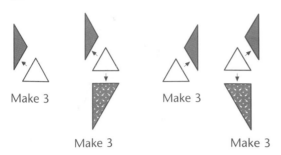

Make 3   Make 3

Make 3   Make 3

3. Join units, adding a triangle unit made in step 1 to complete the half block and reverse half block.

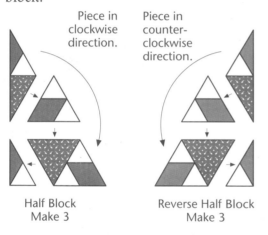

Piece in clockwise direction.

Piece in counter-clockwise direction.

Half Block
Make 3

Reverse Half Block
Make 3

ASSEMBLING THE QUILT

Following the quilt diagram below, arrange the pieced and plain blocks into rows. Sew the rows together, beginning and ending each row with a pieced or plain half block.

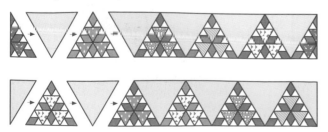

ADDING THE BORDERS

Measure, cut, and sew 2½"-wide borders as directed for "Using Pieced Borders" on pages 96–97.

FINISHING UP

1. Mark quilting lines as desired.
2. Layer the quilt top with batting and backing. Orient the backing seam horizontally. Baste. (See "Basting" on pages 98–99.)
3. Hand or machine quilt. (See "Quilting" on page 100.)
4. Bind the edges. (See "Binding" on pages 100–101.)

Quilting Suggestion

▲ For each pieced block, quilt ¼" inside the small diamonds and quilt a small triangle inside each large triangle.
▲ For each plain block, quilt a diamond grid.
▲ For the border, quilt ¼" from the seams, bind the quilt, then quilt ¼" from the edge of the binding.

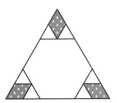

triplicity

COLOR PHOTOS
ON PAGE
35

QUILT SIZE
TWIN: 68½" x 76½"
QUEEN: 85" x 109"

FINISHED BLOCK SIZE
TWIN: 12"
QUEEN: 12"

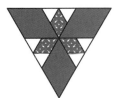

Block A

Block B

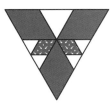

Block D

Unit E

Unit C

NOTE

The pattern for Triplicity is provided in two sizes. The twin size has a plain border, while the border for the queen size is pieced.

Queen

Twin

61

MATERIALS

44"- wide fabric

TWIN

Light	3¼ yds.
Medium 1	½ yd.
Medium 2	½ yd.
Dark	1½ yds.
Backing	4½ yds.
Binding	⅝ yd.

BORDER

Dark	1 yd.

QUEEN

Light	4⅛ yds.
Medium 1	⅝ yd.
Medium 2	⅝ yd.
Dark	2 yds.
Backing	7½ yds.
Binding	*

BORDERS

Light	4⅛ yds.
Medium 1	⅜ yd.
Medium 2	⅜ yd.
Dark	1 yd.

*Binding requirements included in light fabric for border.

CUTTING

Cut the following strips across the width of the fabric from selvage to selvage, then crosscut into the shapes indicated. Refer to "60°-Angle Rotary Cutting," beginning on page 16. The strips without shape designations are used for strip piecing.

TWIN

Note: For inner border, cut 3 strips, each 2½" wide, from the light fabric. For outer border, cut 7 strips, each 4½" wide, from the dark fabric.

Fabric	Strip Width	No. of Strips	No. of Pieces	Shape
Light	21¼"	1	2*	▭
	9¼"	scraps	1	△
	8½"	5	17	⬡
	3¼"	10	—	—
Medium 1	2½"	5	—	—
Medium 2	2½"	5	—	—
Dark	4½"	10	66	▱
Binding	2½"	7	—	—

*Cut 2 rectangles, each 12¼" x 21¼", then cut a 17¼" triangle from the remaining strip.

QUEEN

Note: Cutting instructions for queen-size borders and binding appear on page 65.

Fabric	Strip Width	No. of Strips	No. of Pieces	Shape
Light	21¼"	1	2*	▭
	10"	1	2**	▭
	8½"	7	27	⬡
	3¼"	14	—	—
Medium 1	2½"	7	—	—
Medium 2	2½"	7	—	—
Dark	4½"	15	100	▱

*Cut 2 rectangles, each 12¼" x 21¼", then cut 2 strips, each 4¾" x 21" from the remaining strip. From these strips, cut 14 triangles.
**Cut 2 rectangles, each 10" x 17¼".

ASSEMBLING THE BLOCKS

Block A

1. Sew a 3¼"-wide light strip to a 2½"-wide Medium 1 strip. Cut 2½"-wide segments as shown to make double diamonds. (See "Double Diamonds" on page 21.)

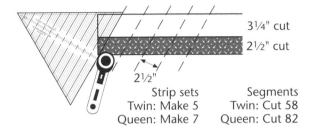

3¼" cut
2½" cut
2½"

Strip sets	Segments
Twin: Make 5	Twin: Cut 58
Queen: Make 7	Queen: Cut 82

2. Sew 2 segments together to make a four-patch unit. Cut each unit into 2 three-patch triangle units, each 4¾" tall. (See "Three-patch Triangles" on pages 21–22.)

   For twin size, reserve 6 triangle units to use later as Unit E. You will have one triangle unit to use for another project.

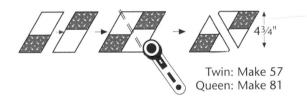

4¾"

Twin: Make 57
Queen: Make 81

3. Sew 3 triangle units to a light hexagon as shown. Press seam allowances toward the hexagon.

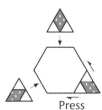

Press

Block A
Twin: Make 17
Queen: Make 27

Block B

1. Sew a 3¼"-wide light strip to a 2½"-wide Medium 2 strip. Cut 2½"-wide segments as shown to make double diamonds.

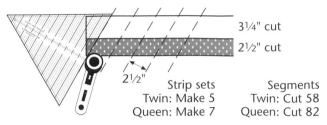

3¼" cut
2½" cut
2½"

Strip sets	Segments
Twin: Make 5	Twin: Cut 58
Queen: Make 7	Queen: Cut 82

2. Sew 2 segments together to make a four-patch unit. Cut each unit into 2 three-patch triangle units, each 4¾" tall.

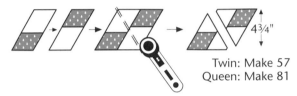

4¾"

Twin: Make 57
Queen: Make 81

3. Sew a dark diamond to opposite sides of the triangle unit. For twin size, set aside 9 of these units to use later as Unit C. For queen size, set aside 11 units to use as Unit C.

Twin: Make 25, reserve 9 for Unit C.
Queen: Make 37, reserve 11 for Unit C.

4. Sew a triangle unit to adjacent sides of a dark diamond. Reserve the extra units in the queen size for Block D.

Twin: Make 16
Queen: Make 26

5. Join units made in steps 3 and 4 to make the number of Block B blocks for your quilt size.

Block B
Twin: Make 16
Queen: Make 18

Block D

1. Sew a 4¾" light triangle between 2 dark diamonds.

Make 8 (Queen)

2. Sew a unit made in step 1 to a reserved unit made in step 4 on page 63.

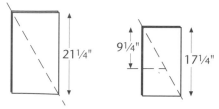

Block D (Queen Only)
Make 8

ASSEMBLING THE QUILT

Edge Triangles

Both sizes: Place the 12¼" x 21¼" rectangles with *wrong sides together.* Cut once diagonally to make 4 half triangles. Place the 10" x 17¼" rectangles with *wrong sides together.* Cut once diagonally to make 4 half triangles. Trim one pair to 9¼".

Twin: Cut a 4¼" triangle from the 60° corner of each of the 17¼" half triangles. (See "Half Triangles" on pages 19–20.)

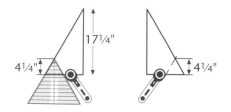

Queen: Add a 4¾" light triangle at one end of each Unit C on row 1. Add a 4¾" light triangle between the C units for row 6.

1. Arrange the blocks and edge pieces in the order shown. Sew rows 1, 2, and 3 together before adding edge triangles. Repeat for rows 4, 5, and 6.

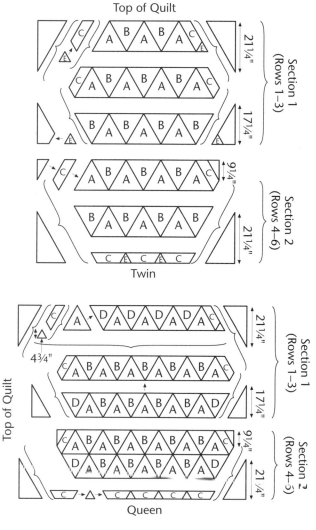

2. Sew the 2 sections together. Press blocks toward dark diamonds as you add to the row.

ADDING THE BORDERS

TWIN

1. Sew the 2½"-wide light strips together, end to end as needed. Measure, cut, and sew top and bottom inner borders to the quilt. (See "Using Plain Borders" on page 95.)
2. Sew the 4½"-wide dark outer border strips together, end to end, as needed. Measure, cut, and sew the side borders to the quilt first, then repeat for top and bottom borders.

QUEEN

Cut the following strips across the width of the fabric from selvage to selvage, then crosscut into the shapes indicated. The strips without shape designations are used for strip piecing.

Fabric	Strip Width	No. of Strips	No. of Pieces	Shape
Light	4⅝"	1*	—	—
	3½"	1**	—	—
	1¹¹⁄₁₆"	12	152***	◁
Medium 1	2½"	3	38	▱
Medium 2	2½"	3	38	▱
Dark	4½"	6	42	▱

*Cut the 4⅝" strip into 4 rectangles, each 8" long. With *wrong sides together,* cut once diagonally to make 8 half triangles.

**Cut the 3½" strip into 4 rectangles, each 6" long. With *wrong sides together,* cut once diagonally to make 8 half triangles.

***Cut half diamonds 5⅞" long. (See "Loose Half Diamonds," page 22.)

Additional Cutting

Cut the following strips *lengthwise* from the remaining light fabric:

4 strips, each 3" wide, for outer border

4 strips, each 2½" wide, for binding

You will also need to cut inner border strips from the light fabric to use as spacer strips after the borders are pieced. See "Spacer Strips" on page 96 and step 6 under "Assembling the Border Blocks" on page 66.

ASSEMBLING THE BORDER BLOCKS

1. Sew a half diamond to 2 sides of each Medium 1 and each Medium 2 small diamond, forming a half-diamond unit.

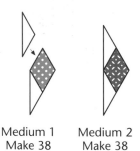

Medium 1
Make 38

Medium 2
Make 38

2. Sew a unit of each color to opposite sides of 34 of the dark diamonds. You will use the remaining pieces to fill in the ends.

Make 34

3. For the top and bottom of the quilt, sew 7 of the units made in step 2 together. Sew 10 units together for each side of the quilt.

Top and bottom borders: 7 units each
Side borders: 10 units each

4. To each end of the border, sew a half-diamond unit to a dark diamond as shown. Sew a small light half triangle, then a large light half triangle to each end to provide the extra fabric necessary to complete the miter. The large light half triangle overlaps the smaller one.

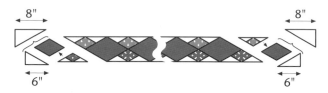

5. At each end of the 4 pieced border strips, determine where you want the miter to begin on the inner edge and mark each point with a pin. Draw the 45° miter line on the wrong side of the pieced border as shown.

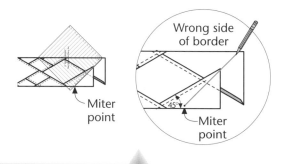

Wrong side of border

Miter point

Miter point

TIP

Choose the miter points so that the points of the dark diamonds meet.

6. *Spacer strips:* If the pieced borders are longer than the edges of the quilt top, make them fit by sewing spacer strips to the quilt, then adding the borders. (See "Spacer Strips" on page 96.) To determine the width of the spacer strip, measure the inner length of the border from miter point to miter point. Measure through the center of the quilt, starting and ending ¼" from each edge (this is where the seam line will be). For spacer strip width, divide the difference between the two measurements in half and add ½" for seam allowances.

mark the border at each edge of the quilt, not including seam allowances.

9. Pin the outer border to the pieced border, matching centers and quarter points. Match pins at the end of the border to the outer end of the miter line drawn on the back of the pieced border. Sew the borders to the quilt, easing if necessary, and mitering the corners.

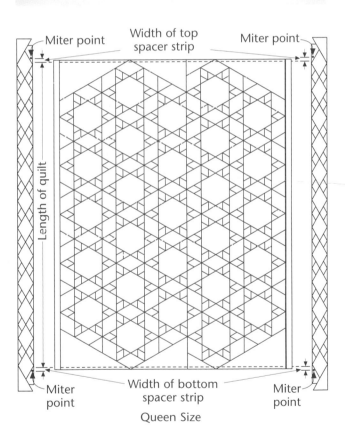

Queen Size

7. Pin all four pieced border strips to the quilt, matching centers, quarter points, and ends. Sew the borders to the quilt, easing where necessary. Miter the corners. (See "Mitering Corners" on page 97.)

8. Place the 3"-wide outer border strip along the center of the quilt. Mark center and quarter points of the border with pins. Place a pin to

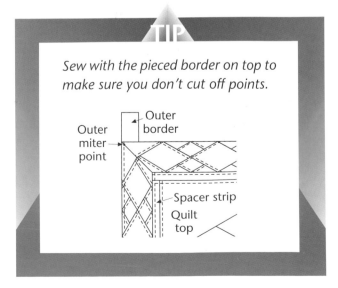

FINISHING UP

1. Mark quilting lines as desired.
2. Layer the quilt top with batting and backing. For both quilt sizes, orient the backing seam horizontally. Baste. (See "Basting" on pages 98–99.)

3. Hand or machine quilt. (See "Quilting" on page 100.)
4. Bind the edges. (See "Binding" on pages 100–101.)

Quilting Suggestion

▲ Quilt ¼" inside the seam line of the small diamonds.
▲ Quilt the large diamonds with an arch from point to point.

▲ Quilt the scallop and flower design on page 69 in each light hexagon.
▲ For the queen size, echo quilt lines ¾" apart along spacer and outer borders.
▲ For the twin-size quilt, fill the background next to the border with a freehand flowering vine or clamshell design. Continue the clamshell design out into the border or use a design from a commercial quilting stencil.

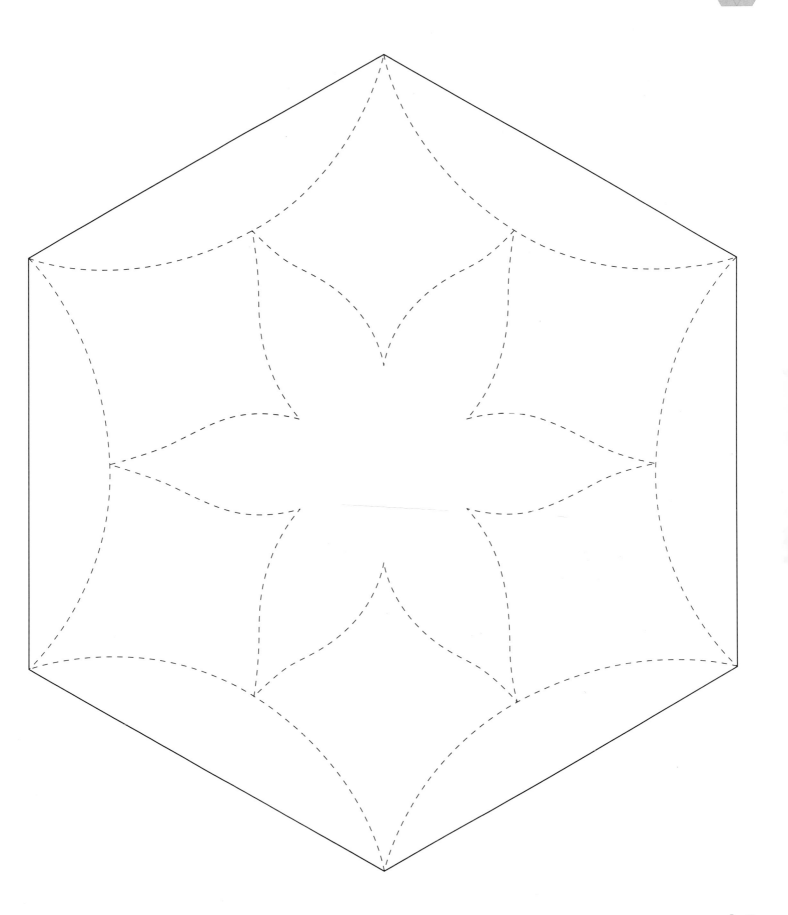

trio of triangles

COLOR PHOTOS
ON PAGES
38–39

QUILT SIZE
69½" x 73½"

FINISHED BLOCK SIZE
12"

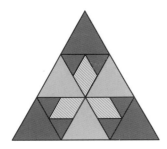

Block A

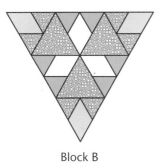

Block B

MATERIALS
44"- wide fabric

1⅞ yds. dark aqua
½ yd. light aqua
1⅜ yds. dark pink
⅝ yd. light pink
2½ yds. dark blue
⅝ yd. light blue
⅝ yd. for binding
4¼ yds. for backing

CUTTING

Cut the following strips across the width of the fabric from selvage to selvage, then crosscut into the shapes indicated. Refer to "60°-Angle Rotary Cutting," beginning on page 16. The strips without shape designations are used for strip piecing.

Note: For inner borders, cut 7 strips, each 2½" wide, from the dark aqua fabric. For outer borders, cut 7 strips, each 5" wide, from the dark blue fabric.

Fabric	Strip Width	No. of Strips	No. of Pieces	Shape
Dark aqua	4¾"	5	58	△
	3¼"	5	—	—
	3"	1	2*	▭
Light aqua	2½"	5	—	—
	1¹¹⁄₁₆"	1	4**	◁
Dark pink	4¾"	5	58	△
	3¼"	6	—	—
	3"	1	2*	▭
Light pink	2½"	6	—	—
	1¹¹⁄₁₆"	1	6**	◁
Dark blue	4¾"	5	57	△
	3¼"	6	—	—
	3"	1	4*	▭
Light blue	2½"	6	—	—
	1¹¹⁄₁₆"	1	6**	◁
Binding	2½"	7	—	—

*Cut each rectangle 3" x 5¼". With rectangles *wrong sides together*, cut once diagonally to make half triangles. Trim remainder of the 3"-wide strip to 2¾" wide and cut the following number of triangles: dark aqua: 4, dark pink: 6, dark blue: 6.
**Cut half diamonds 5⅞" long. (See "Loose Half Diamonds," page 22.)

ASSEMBLING THE BLOCKS

Block A

1. Sew a 3¼"-wide dark aqua strip to a 2½"-wide light aqua strip. Cut 2½"-wide segments to make double-diamond units. (See "Double Diamonds" on page 21).

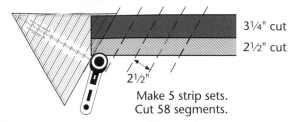

3¼" cut
2½" cut
2½"

Make 5 strip sets.
Cut 58 segments.

2. Sew 2 segments together to make a four-patch unit. Cut each unit into 2 three-patch triangle units, each 4¾" tall. (See "Three-Patch Triangles" on pages 21–22.)

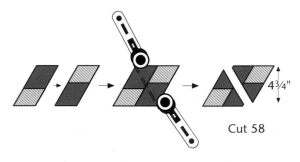

4¾"

Cut 58

3. Sew a dark aqua triangle to each aqua three-patch triangle unit.

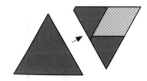

Make 58

4. Sew a diamond unit made in step 3 to 2 adjacent sides of a dark pink triangle.

Make 18

5. Sew a dark pink triangle to 2 adjacent sides of a diamond unit, then sew to the unit made in step 4. Press seam allowances toward the triangles.

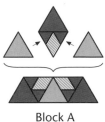

Block A
Make 18

Half Block A and Reverse Half Block A

1. Sew a 2¾" dark aqua triangle to a light aqua half diamond. Add a dark aqua half triangle, forming a larger half diamond.

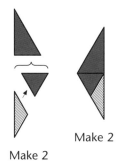

Make 2

Make 2

2. Add a dark pink triangle, a diamond unit, then a dark pink half triangle.

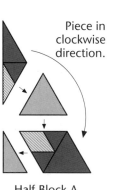

Piece in clockwise direction.

Piece in counter-clockwise direction.

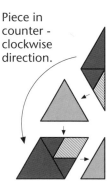

Half Block A
Make 2

Reverse Half Block A
Make 2

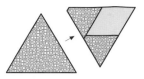

Block B

1. Sew a 3¼"-wide dark pink strip to a 2½"-wide light pink strip. Cut 2½"-wide segments to make double-diamond units.

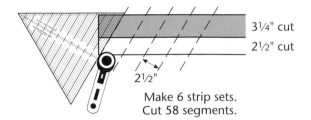

3¼" cut
2½" cut

2½"

Make 6 strip sets.
Cut 58 segments.

2. Sew 2 segments together to make a four-patch unit. Cut each unit into 2 three-patch triangle units, each 4¾" tall.

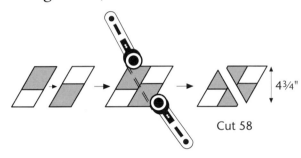

4¾"

Cut 58

3. Sew a 3¼"-wide dark blue strip to a 2½"-wide light blue strip. Cut 2½"-wide segments to make double-diamond units.

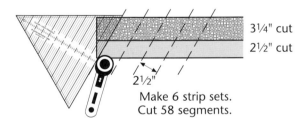

3¼" cut
2½" cut

2½"

Make 6 strip sets.
Cut 58 segments.

4. Sew 2 segments together to make a four-patch unit. Cut each unit into 2 three-patch triangle units, each 4¾" tall.

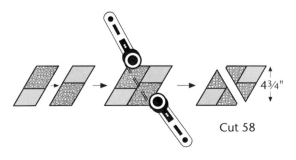

4¾"

Cut 58

5. Sew a dark blue triangle to each blue three-patch triangle unit.

Make 57

6. Sew a blue unit made in step 5 to 2 adjacent sides of a pink triangle unit made in step 2.

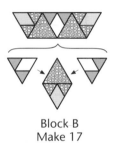

Make 17

7. Sew a pink triangle unit to 2 adjacent sides of a blue unit, then sew to the unit made in step 6. Press seam allowances toward the blue units.

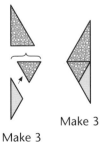

Block B
Make 17

Half Block B and Reverse Half Block B

1. Sew a 2¾" dark blue triangle to a light blue half diamond. Add a dark blue half triangle, forming a half-diamond unit.

Make 3

Make 3

73

2. Sew a 2¾" dark pink triangle to a light pink half diamond, then sew to the blue diamond unit made in step 5 of Block B. Add a pink triangle unit from step 2 of Block B, then a blue half-diamond from step 1.

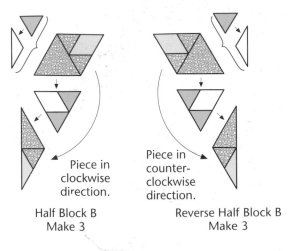

Piece in clockwise direction.

Piece in counter-clockwise direction.

Half Block B
Make 3

Reverse Half Block B
Make 3

ASSEMBLING THE QUILT

Following the quilt diagram below, sew the blocks into rows. Sew the rows together.

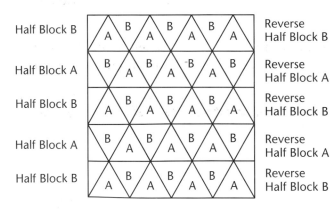

Half Block B	Reverse Half Block B
Half Block A	Reverse Half Block A
Half Block B	Reverse Half Block B
Half Block A	Reverse Half Block A
Half Block B	Reverse Half Block B

ADDING THE BORDERS

1. Join 2½"-wide dark inner border strips as needed. Measure, cut, and sew the side borders, then the top and bottom borders to the quilt. (See "Using Plain Borders," page 95.)
2. Repeat step 1 for the 5" dark blue outer border.

FINISHING UP

1. Mark quilting lines as desired.
2. Layer the quilt top with batting and backing. Orient the backing seam horizontally. Baste. (See "Basting" on pages 98–99.)
3. Hand or machine quilt. (See "Quilting" on page 100.)
4. Bind the edges. (See "Binding" on pages 100–101.)

Quilting Suggestion

▲ Emphasize each triangle by quilting each color differently.
▲ Quilt the border with 30°-angle lines 2" apart.

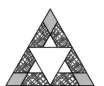

magic jewels

COLOR PHOTO
ON PAGE
40

QUILT SIZE
42½" x 49½"

FINISHED BLOCK SIZE
9"

Block A

Block B

Block C

Block D

MATERIALS

44"- wide fabric

½ yd. light gold

¼ yd. dark gold

1½ yds. dark leaf print for blocks, border, and binding

¼ yd. purple

¾ yd. lavender

2⅝ yds. for backing

CUTTING

Cut the following strips across the width of the fabric from selvage to selvage, then crosscut into the shapes indicated. Refer to "60°-Angle Rotary Cutting," beginning on page 16. The strips without shape designation are used for strip piecing.

Note: For the border, cut 6 strips, each 3½" wide, from the dark leaf print. For the binding, cut 4 strips, each 2½" wide, from the dark leaf print.

Fabric	Strip Width	No. of Strips	No. of Pieces	Shape
Light gold	5¼"	1	12	△
	2¼"	2	36	△
Dark gold	2"	2	24	▱
Dark leaf print	2"	4	48*	⬡
	2"	3	48	▱
Purple	2"	2	—	—
Lavender	2¾"	2	—	—
	5"	3	12**	⬡
	2¼"	1	12	△

*Cut dark trapezoids with lower edge of strip on the ruler's 3¾" mark.
**Cut lavender trapezoids with lower edge of strip on the ruler's 9¾" mark. (See "Trapezoids" on page 24.)

ASSEMBLING THE BLOCKS

Blocks A and B

1. Sew a dark leaf print trapezoid to a dark gold diamond.

Make 24

2. Sew a 2¼" lavender triangle to a dark leaf print trapezoid. Sew a 2¼" light gold triangle to each of the 18 remaining dark leaf print trapezoids.

Make 6   Make 18   2¼"

3. Sew a unit made in step 2 to a unit made in step 1.

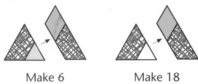

Make 6   Make 18

4. Sew a lavender triangle unit to the top of a large lavender trapezoid.

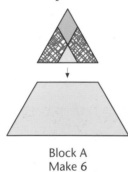

Block A
Make 6

5. Sew a light gold triangle unit to each side of a 5¼" light gold triangle.

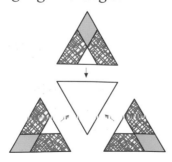

Block B
Make 6

Blocks C and D

1. Sew a 2"-wide purple strip to a 2¾"-wide lavender strip. Cut 2"-wide segments as shown to make double-diamond units. (See "Double Diamonds" on page 21.)

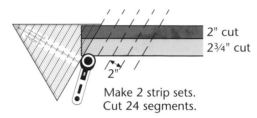

2" cut
2¾" cut
2"

Make 2 strip sets.
Cut 24 segments.

2. Sew 2 segments together to make a four-patch unit. Cut each four-patch unit into 2 three-patch triangle units. (See "Three-Patch Triangles" on pages 21–22.)

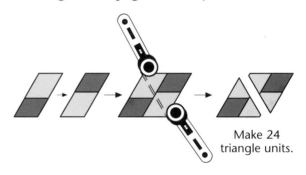

Make 24
triangle units.

3. Sew a dark leaf print diamond to 2 sides of a 2¼" lavender triangle and to 2 sides of a 2¼" light gold triangle.

Make 6   Make 18

4. Sew a unit made in step 2 to a unit made in step 3.

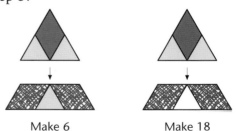

Make 6   Make 18

5. Sew a triangle unit with 3 lavender triangles to the top of a large lavender trapezoid.

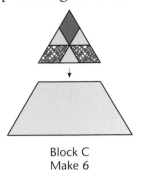

Block C
Make 6

6. Sew a triangle unit with 2 lavender triangles to each side of a 5¼" light gold triangle.

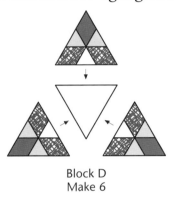

Block D
Make 6

Assembling The Quilt

1. Sew the blocks together to make the 2 different sections shown below.

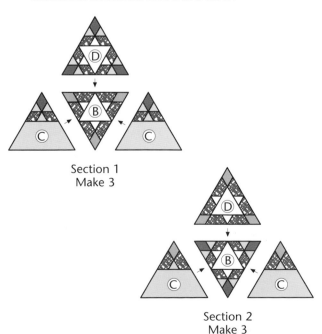

Section 1
Make 3

Section 2
Make 3

2. For the border, sew a 3½"-wide dark leaf print border strip to the lavender trapezoid side of each section, extending the strip at least 3" beyond the corners of the section. Align the edge of a ruler along the edge of the section to trim each end of the border, continuing the angle of the section.

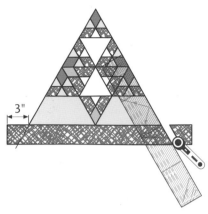

3. Sew 3 sections together, alternating sections 1 and 2, then join the other 3 sections. Join the 2 halves.

Finishing Up

1. Mark quilting lines as desired.
2. Layer the quilt top with batting and backing. Baste. (See "Basting" on pages 98–99.)
3. Hand or machine quilt. (See "Quilting" on page 100.)
4. Bind the edges. (See "Binding" on pages 100–101.)

Quilting Suggestion

▲ Quilt ¼" inside the shapes as shown.

▲ Quilt the leaf design in each background trapezoid.

▲ Quilt ¼" inside the seams for the border. After binding the quilt, quilt ¼" from the border's outer edge.

star flurries

COLOR PHOTOS
ON PAGE
29

QUILT SIZE
80½" x 88"

FINISHED BLOCK SIZE
9"

Block A

Block B

Unit C

Unit D

Unit E

Unit F

MATERIALS

44"-wide fabric

2¾ yds. cream for
background

1⅜ yds. medium pink

1⅛ yds. medium rust

1⅛ yds. medium brown

2⅛ yds. dark pink for blocks
and outer border

¾ yd. dark rust

2 yds. dark brown for blocks,
inner border, and binding

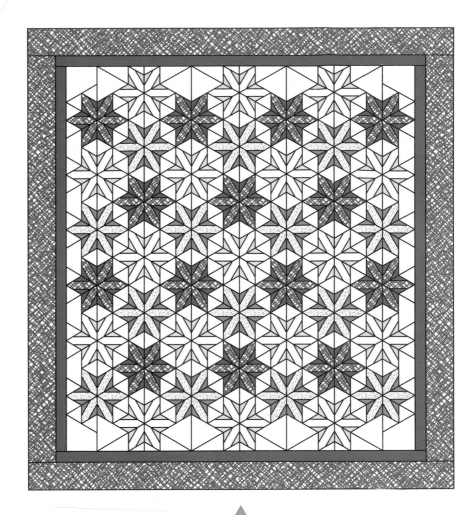

CUTTING

Cut the following strips across the width of the fabric from selvage to selvage, then crosscut into the shapes indicated. Refer to "60°-Angle Rotary Cutting," beginning on page 16. Some of the strips in the chart below have additional cutting requirements. See "Additional Cutting" on page 80.

Note: For the inner border, cut 8 strips, each 2½" wide, from the dark brown fabric. For the outer border, cut 8 strips, each 5½" wide, from the dark pink fabric. For the binding, cut 9 strips, each 2½" wide, from the dark brown fabric.

Fabric	Strip Width	No. of Strips	No. of Pieces	Shape
Cream	3¾"	15	244	△
	6¾"	2	—	—
	7¼"	1	—	—
	6½"	1	4	▱
	3½"	2	—	—

Additional Cutting

From the 6¾"-wide strips, cut 12 triangles. Trim the remainder of the second strip to 4¼" wide and cut 6 more triangles. Bisect the 4¼" triangle to make 6 half triangles and 6 reverse half triangles.

From the 7¼"-wide strip, cut 6 triangles. Bisect these to make 6 half triangles and 6 reverse half triangles.

From the 3½"-wide strips, cut 10 trapezoids with lower edge of strip on the ruler's 6¾" mark.

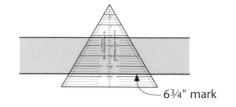

6¾" mark

Cut strips, following the chart below, then subcut into diamonds.

Fabric	Strip Width	No. of Strips	No. of Diamonds
Medium pink	3½"	12	102
Medium rust	3½"	10	84
Medium brown	3½"	10	84
Dark pink	2"	13	204
Dark rust	2"	11	168
Dark brown	2"	11	168

ASSEMBLING THE BLOCKS

1. Using a pen or light-colored marking pencil, draw a vertical line from point to point on the wrong side of all the 2" dark pink, dark rust, and dark brown diamonds.

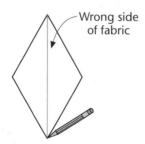

Wrong side of fabric

over itself, checking to make sure all cut edges are even.

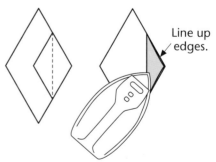

Line up edges.

2. Place a 2" diamond, right sides together, on top of a 3½" diamond as shown above right. Match the dark diamonds with the medium diamonds of the same color. Stitch on the drawn line. Press the small diamond back

NOTE

Stitch only a few of these at first to verify that the edges are lined up correctly. If necessary, adjust your line of stitching to the right or left of the pencil line.

3. Continue chain piecing a small diamond to each of the large diamonds. (See "Chain Piecing" on pages 27–28.) Press and check the edges for accuracy, then trim the extra fabric, leaving a ¼"-wide seam allowance.

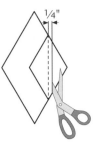

4. Chain-piece a matching small diamond to the opposite side of each large diamond. Press and trim.

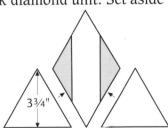

Medium pink/
Dark pink
Make 102

Medium rust/
Dark rust
Make 84

Medium brown/
Dark brown
Make 84

5. Sew a 3¾" cream triangle to 2 adjacent sides of a pink diamond unit. Set aside 4 to make Unit D.

Make 70
Reserve 4 for Unit D.

> ### NOTE
>
> *My variation is a controlled scrap quilt using pink, rust, and brown. I found it easiest to arrange only the diamond units on a flannel wall, keeping the cream triangles at the sewing machine. By sewing all the A blocks in a row, and all the B blocks in a row, I was able to quickly sew the blocks in the correct order.*

6. **Block A:** Sew a rust diamond unit to the left side and a brown diamond unit to the right side of a 3¾" cream triangle. Add a pink diamond unit made in step 5.

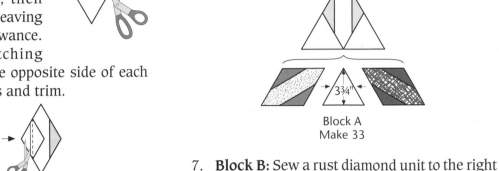

Block A
Make 33

7. **Block B:** Sew a rust diamond unit to the right side and a brown diamond unit to the left side of a 3¾" cream triangle. Add a pink diamond unit made in step 5.

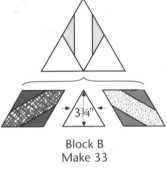

Block B
Make 33

8. **Unit C:** Sew a 3¾" cream triangle between 2 diamond units, following the diagram below, then sew a cream trapezoid to the top of each unit.

Pink   Rust
Make 2

Rust   Pink
Make 2

Brown   Pink
Make 2

Pink   Brown
Make 2

Rust   Brown
Make 1

Brown   Rust
Make 1

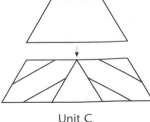

Unit C
Make 10

9. **Unit D:** Sew a 3¾" cream triangle to 2 adjacent sides of a diamond unit.

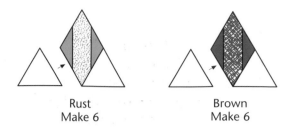

Rust
Make 6

Brown
Make 6

10. **Unit E:** Sew a 3¾" cream triangle between 2 diamond units, following the diagram below, then sew a 6¾" cream triangle to the top of each unit.

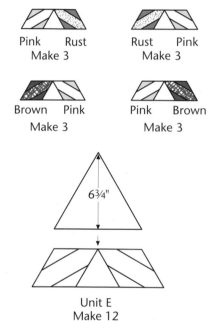

Pink   Rust
Make 3

Rust   Pink
Make 3

Brown   Pink
Make 3

Pink   Brown
Make 3

6¾"

Unit E
Make 12

11. **Unit F:** Sew a 7¼" cream half triangle to one side, and a 4¼" cream half triangle to the adjacent side of a pink diamond unit.

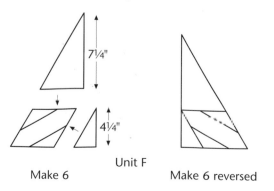

7¼"

4¼"

Unit F

Make 6

Make 6 reversed

ASSEMBLING THE QUILT

1. Arrange the blocks and half blocks in the order shown. Turn the blocks as needed to match star colors. Sew into rows. Sew a 6½" cream diamond to each corner, orienting them so that there are no bias edges at the corner when trimmed.

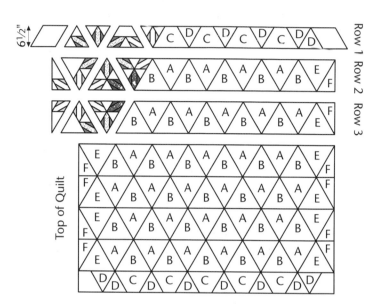

6½"

Top of Quilt

Row 1   Row 2   Row 3

NOTE

The quilt diagram above is shown on its side with the top of the quilt at left. Refer to the diagram below for correct orientation of D blocks when placing them into the row.

2. Sew rows together; trim corners square.

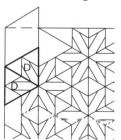
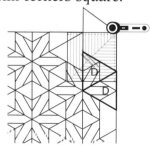

Upper Left and Lower Right Corners

Upper Right and Lower Left Corners

82

ADDING THE BORDERS

1. For each side, join 2 dark brown inner border strips, each 2½" wide. Measure, cut, and sew side borders to the quilt first, then repeat for the top and bottom borders. (See "Using Plain Borders" on page 95.)
2. Join 5½"-wide dark pink outer border strips as needed. Measure, cut, and sew borders to the sides, then to the top and bottom of the quilt.

FINISHING UP

1. Mark quilting lines as desired.
2. Layer the quilt top with batting and backing. Orient the backing seam vertically. Baste. (See "Basting" on pages 98–99.)
3. Hand or machine quilt. (See "Quilting" on page 100.)
4. Bind the edges. (See "Binding" on pages 100–101.)

Quilting Suggestion

▲ Quilt a Y in each diamond unit as shown. They should connect, forming a small star in the center of each larger star.
▲ Quilt the design provided below for the cream triangles between stars.
▲ Quilt a single cable design in the inner border, and a double cable in the outer border.

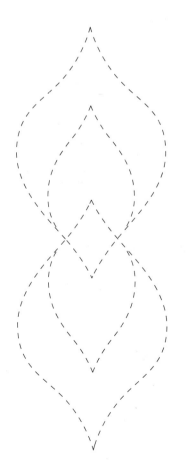

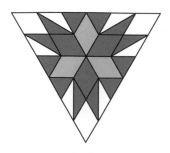

cosmic columbines

COLOR PHOTO
ON PAGE
34

QUILT SIZE
54" x 59"

FINISHED BLOCK SIZE
9"

Block A

Block B

MATERIALS
44"- wide fabric

1⅝ yds. dark blue

⅜ yd. light blue

½ yd. medium pink for center triangles

1 yd. light pink

1¾ yds. dark red for diamonds, outer border, and binding

⅞ yd. medium red for diamonds and inner border

3½ yds. for backing

CUTTING

Cut the following strips across the width of the fabric from selvage to selvage, then crosscut into the shapes indicated. Refer to "60°-Angle Rotary Cutting," beginning on page 16. The strips without shape designations are used for strip piecing.

Note: For the inner border, cut 5 strips, each 1½" wide, from the medium red fabric. For the outer border, cut 6 strips, each 4½" wide, from the dark red fabric. For the binding, cut 6 strips, each 2½" wide, from the dark red fabric.

BLOCK A

Fabric	Strip Width	No. of Strips	No. of Pieces	Shape
Dark blue	2"	4	57	▱
	2¾"	4	—	—
	1¾"	8	—	—
	2¼"	1	6*	△
Light blue	2"	4	—	—
	1⅜"	1	6**	◁
Light pink	2"	4	57	▱
	1¾"	8	—	—
	2¼"	1	4*	△

*Cut triangles, then trim strip to 1⅜" and cut 6 half diamonds, each 4⅞" long. Reserve the 4 light pink triangles for the top row.
**Cut half diamonds 4⅞" long.

BLOCK B

Fabric	Strip Width	No. of Strips	No. of Pieces	Shape
Dark red	2"	5	—	—
	1⅜"	1	4*	◁
Medium red	2"	5	—	—
	2"	4	62	▱
Dark blue	2"	6	67**	⬓
Med. pink	5¼"	2	18	△
	3⅜"	1	2***	▭

*Cut half diamonds 4⅞" long.
**Cut trapezoids with lower edge of strip on the ruler's 3¾" mark. Reserve 5 for top row.

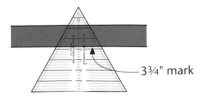

3¾" mark

***Cut rectangles 5¾" long. With *wrong sides together*, cut diagonally to make 2 reverse and 2 half triangles.

ASSEMBLING THE BLOCKS

Block A

1. Alternating the 1¾"-wide dark blue strips with the 1¾"-wide light pink strips, sew together to make a strip-pieced panel. Press seam allowances toward the dark blue strips. Cut 4" half-diamond units. (See "Strip-Pieced Half Diamonds" on page 23.)

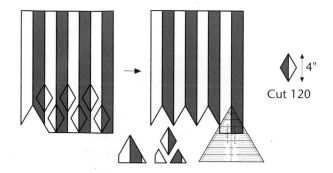

Cut 120

2. Sew a half-diamond unit made in step 1 to a 2" light pink diamond, and a half-diamond unit to a 2" dark blue diamond. Following the diagram below, sew these 2 units together to make a diamond unit.

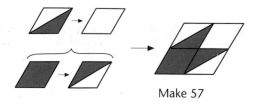

Make 57

3. Sew a 2"-wide light blue strip to a 2¾"-wide dark blue strip. Cut 2"-wide segments as shown to make double-diamond units. (See "Double Diamonds" on page 21.)

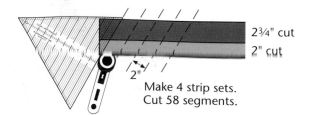

2¾" cut
2" cut
2"
Make 4 strip sets.
Cut 58 segments.

4. Sew 2 segments together to make a four-patch unit. Cut each unit into 2 three-patch triangle units. (See "Three-Patch Triangles" on pages 21–22.)

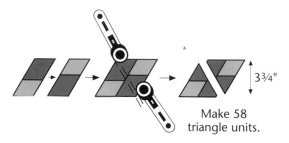

3¾"

Make 58 triangle units.

5. Sew a diamond unit made in step 2 to 2 adjacent sides of a triangle unit made in step 4.

Make 17

6. Sew a triangle unit made in step 4 to 2 adjacent sides of a diamond unit made in step 2, then sew to the unit made in step 5.

Block A
Make 17

Half Block A and Half Block A Reversed

1. Sew a 2¼" dark blue triangle to a 4⅞" light blue half diamond as shown.

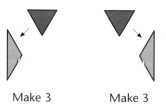

Make 3   Make 3

2. Sew a 4⅞" dark blue half diamond and a 4⅞" light pink half diamond to the dark sides of a half-diamond unit made in step 1 of Block A.

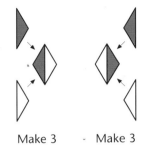

Make 3   Make 3

3. Join units made in steps 1 and 2 with diamond and triangle units units to complete Half Block A and Half Block A Reversed.

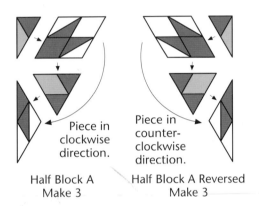

Piece in clockwise direction.

Piece in counter-clockwise direction.

Half Block A
Make 3

Half Block A Reversed
Make 3

Block B

1. Sew a 2"-wide dark red strip to a 2"-wide medium red strip. Cut 42 double-diamond segments, each 2" wide. (See "Double Diamonds" on page 21.) Turn the remainder of the strip sets over and cut 24 double-diamond segments, each 2" wide.

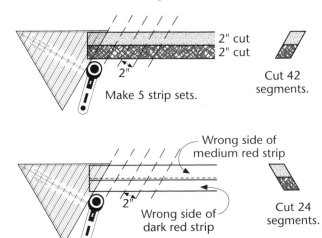

2" cut
2" cut
2"
Make 5 strip sets.

Cut 42 segments.

Wrong side of medium red strip
2"
Wrong side of dark red strip
Cut 24 segments.

2. Sew a medium red diamond to each end of a dark blue trapezoid. Reserve 4 to make the half blocks.

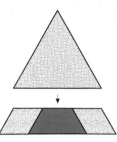

Make 22; reserve 4.

3. Sew a trapezoid unit to a 5¼" medium pink triangle.

Make 18

4. Sew a double-diamond unit made in step 1 to the right end of a dark blue trapezoid, and sew a medium red diamond to the left end of the trapezoid. Sew this unit to a 5¼" medium pink triangle unit made in step 3.

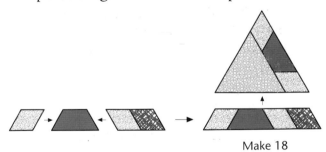

Make 18

5. Sew a double-diamond unit made in step 1 to each end of a dark blue trapezoid. Sew this unit to the unit made in step 4 as shown.

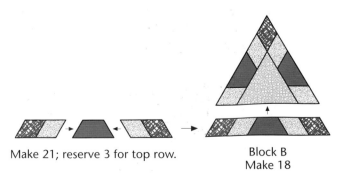

Make 21; reserve 3 for top row.

Block B
Make 18

87

Half Block B and Half Block B Reversed

1. Sew a dark red half diamond to the end of a unit reserved from step 2 of Block B. Sew to the medium pink half triangles.

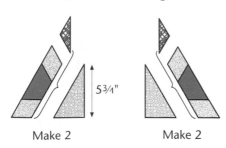

Make 2   Make 2

2. Sew a double-diamond unit made in step 1 of Block B to a dark blue trapezoid. Sew this unit to the half-triangle unit made in step 1. Press. Trim off the portion of the trapezoid extending beyond the half triangle.

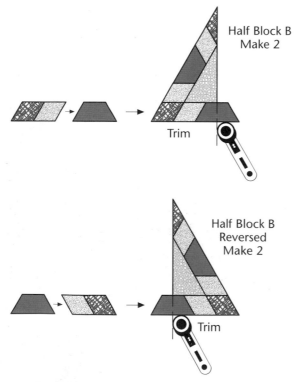

Half Block B
Make 2

Trim

Half Block B
Reversed
Make 2

Trim

3. Referring to the illustration below, sew a 2" light pink triangle between the reserved units made in step 5 of Block B, alternating 4 triangles with 3 units. Sew a remaining strip-pieced diamond unit and a dark blue trapezoid to each end as shown.

ASSEMBLING THE QUILT

1. Following the quilt diagram, assemble blocks into rows, beginning and ending with half blocks and alternating A and B blocks. Sew the rows together.

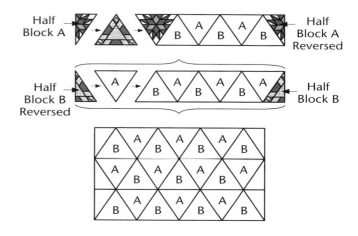

Half Block A →   ← Half Block A Reversed

Half Block B Reversed →   ← Half Block B

2. Add the top row and trim the trapezoids at each end square with the quilt top.

Top row

88

ADDING THE BORDERS

1. Join 1½"-wide medium red inner border strips as needed. Measure, cut, and sew a border to each side of the quilt, then to the top and bottom. (See "Using Plain Borders" on page 95.)
2. Join 4½"-wide dark red outer border strips as needed. Measure, cut, and sew borders to the sides of the quilt, then to the top and bottom.

FINISHING UP

1. Mark quilting lines as desired.
2. Layer the quilt top with batting and backing. Orient the backing seam horizontally. Baste. (See "Basting" on pages 98–99.)
3. Hand or machine quilt. (See "Quilting" on page 100.)
4. Bind the edges. (See "Binding" on pages 100–101.)

Quilting Suggestion

▲ Quilt the columbines with lines from the center of the block to the point of each half diamond.

▲ Quilt ¼" inside the shape formed by the dark blue trapezoid and triangles.

▲ Quilt ¼" inside the seam for the dark and medium red diamonds.

▲ Quilt the design provided below left in the medium pink triangles.

▲ Quilt a cable design in the outer border.

desert ice

COLOR PHOTO
ON PAGE
40

QUILT SIZE
30½" x 35½"

FINISHED BLOCK SIZE
10½"

MATERIALS
44"-wide fabric

¼ yd. Color 1 (dark orange)

⅓ yd. Color 2 (medium orange)

¼ yd. Color 3 (medium peach)

⅓ yd. Color 4 (light peach)

⅛ yd. Color 5 (medium gold)

⅛ yd. Color 6 (dark gold)

⅓ yd. Color 7 (light gold)

¼ yd. green print

1⅓ yds. dark green for blocks and binding

1 yd. for backing

CUTTING

Cut the following strips across the width of the fabric from selvage to selvage, then crosscut into the shapes indicated. Refer to "60°-Angle Rotary Cutting," beginning on page 16. The strips without shape designations are used for strip piecing.

Note: For binding, cut 3 strips, each 2¼" wide, from the dark green fabric.

Fabric	Strip Width	No. of Strips	No. of Pieces	Shape
Color 1	1¾"	2	—	—
Color 2	1¾"	2	—	—
	2"	1	6	▱
Color 3	1¾"	2	—	—
Color 4	2"	3	24*	⬯
Color 5	1¾"	1	—	—
Color 6	2"	1	12	▱
Color 7	2"	3	—	—
	2"	1	6*	⬯
	1¾"	1	—	—
Green print	6¾"	1	6	△
Dark green	1¾"	10	—	—
	2"	4	60	▱
	2¼"	1	12	△

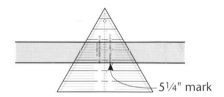

5¼" mark

*Cut trapezoids with lower edge of strip on the ruler's 5¼" mark.

ASSEMBLING THE BLOCKS

1. Using a pen or light-colored marking pencil, draw a vertical line from point to point on the wrong side of all of the dark green diamonds.

Wrong side of dark green diamond

2. Place a dark green diamond, right sides together, over one corner of each Color 4 (light peach) and Color 7 (light gold) trapezoid. Match all three edges exactly. Stitch on the line. Press the small diamond back over itself and check that all cut edges are even.

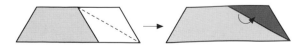

NOTE

Stitch only a few diamonds at first to verify that the edges are lined up correctly. If necessary, adjust your line of stitching to the right or left of the drawn line.

3. Continue chain-piecing the dark green diamonds to the trapezoids. (See "Chain Piecing" on pages 27–28.) Press, then trim the extra fabric, leaving a ¼"-wide seam allowance.

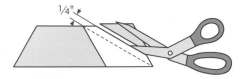

4. Chain-piece a matching dark green diamond to the adjacent corner of each trapezoid. Press and trim.

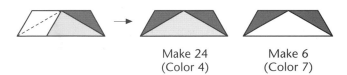

Make 24
(Color 4)

Make 6
(Color 7)

5. Sew 2 panels of 1¾" strips, alternating dark green strips with the color strips in the order shown below. If desired, press seams open to distribute bulk.

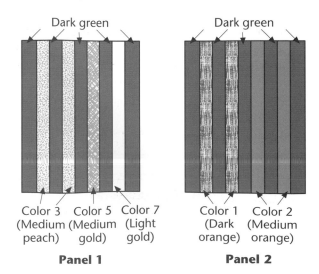

Color 3
(Medium peach)

Color 5
(Medium gold)

Color 7
(Light gold)

Panel 1

Color 1
(Dark orange)

Color 2
(Medium orange)

Panel 2

6. Cut the number of 4" half-diamond units from the panels as indicated below. (See "Strip-Pieced Half Diamonds" on page 23.)

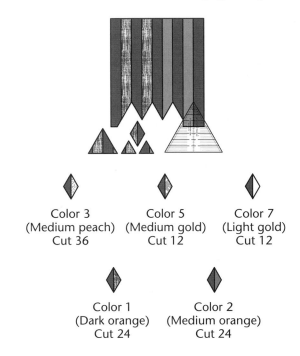

Color 3
(Medium peach)
Cut 36

Color 5
(Medium gold)
Cut 12

Color 7
(Light gold)
Cut 12

Color 1
(Dark orange)
Cut 24

Color 2
(Medium orange)
Cut 24

7. Sew a Color 3 and a Color 5 half-diamond unit made in step 6 to each end of 6 of the Color 4 trapezoid units made in step 4, referring to the diagram below for the correct color placement. Press seam allowances away from the trapezoid unit.

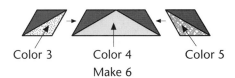

Color 3   Color 4   Color 5

Make 6

8. Sew a Color 5 and Color 3 half-diamond unit to each end of 6 of the Color 4 trapezoid units, referring to the diagram below for correct color placement. Sew a Color 2 diamond to the right end of this unit.

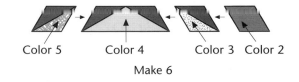

Color 5   Color 4   Color 3   Color 2

Make 6

9. Sew a Color 7 half-diamond unit to each end of a Color 7 trapezoid unit. Sew a Color 6 diamond to each end as shown.

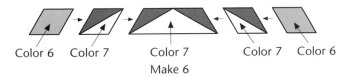

Color 6　Color 7　Color 7
Make 6
Color 7　Color 6

10. Sew the trapezoid unit made in step 7 to one side of a 6¾" green print triangle. Press seam allowances toward the large triangle.

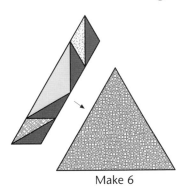

Make 6

11. Sew the trapezoid unit made in step 8, then the trapezoid unit made in step 9 to the remaining sides of the green print triangle.

Make 6

ADDING THE BORDERS

1. Sew a 2"-wide Color 7 strip to the Color 7 trapezoid unit added in step 11 above, extending the strip at least 2" beyond the edge of the triangle. Trim each end of the strip

to the same angle as the triangle. Press the seam allowances toward the strip. Repeat for remaining units, sewing and trimming strips.

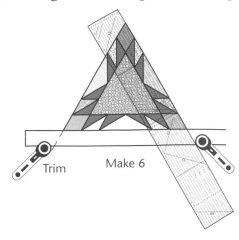

Trim　Make 6

2. Assemble the pieced inner and outer border strips, using the remaining half-diamond and trapezoid units. Refer to the diagram below for the correct color order. Press seam allowances for outer border strip in the opposite direction from the inner border strip's seam allowances. Sew a 2¼" dark green triangle to each end of the outer border strip.

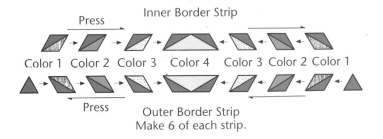

Press　Inner Border Strip

Color 1　Color 2　Color 3　Color 4　Color 3　Color 2　Color 1

Press　Outer Border Strip
Make 6 of each strip.

3. Sew inner and outer border strips together. Press the seam allowances for 3 border strips toward the inner border strip, and the seam allowances for the remaining border strips toward the outer border strip.

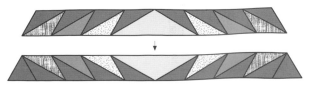

Make 6

4. Sew a border strip to the strip added in step 1 to complete each triangle block.

Make 6

5. Sew 6 triangle blocks together to complete the top. Alternate blocks with border seams lying in opposite directions to distribute the bulk. Press the seams between blocks open.

FINISHING UP

1. Mark quilting lines as desired.
2. Layer the quilt top with batting and backing. Baste. (See "Basting" on pages 98–99.)
3. Hand or machine quilt. (See "Quilting" on page 100.)
4. Bind the edges. (See "Binding" on pages 100–101.)

Quilting Suggestion

▲ Quilt ¼" inside the edge of the small diamonds and large triangles.
▲ Quilt a V through the center of each "arrow."
▲ Quilt the design below inside the large light diamonds.

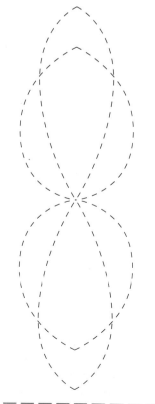

ADDING BORDERS

I recommend including at least one border around the edge of the quilt. Not only does the border frame the quilt; it contains the movement of the design. Choose a border that complements the body of the quilt rather than calls attention to itself.

Almost all piecing places some bias on at least two edges of the quilt. A narrow, plain, or unobtrusive border of the background fabric stabilizes the bias. Of course, a wider border (or two or three borders) might look even better.

Borders once were my problem area in quiltmaking. They were wavy and wouldn't lie flat. They seemed to have stretched out of shape during the quilting stage.

Then I learned that the best way to avoid a wavy border is to measure and cut the border the exact length first rather than sewing it to the quilt top and cutting off the extra. Sewing the border strips to the top without measuring properly can easily add three or more inches to the length. This extra fullness is not easily quilted out.

Adding the border is nearly your last chance to square up the quilt top. If you are making the quilt for competition or a wall, it is even more important to end up with a properly squared quilt in which opposite sides are the same length. In competition, it is not unusual to see a judge fold the quilts in half to check for this.

USING PLAIN BORDERS

For flat, smooth borders, first cut the required number of strips to go around the perimeter of the quilt. Remove the selvages from the ends of the strips with a perpendicular cut. Use a ¼"-wide seam to join the border strips into a strip of sufficient length for each side. (I like to cut and join

two opposite sides at a time.) Be sure to backstitch these seams and press them open so they lie flatter and are less conspicuous. Try to place the seams randomly around the quilt, making them even less noticeable.

Measure for side borders through the center of the quilt top from the top to bottom edges. I smooth the smaller quilt tops onto my flannel wall and hold the border strip up to the center to find the length. I often work on the floor with the large quilts.

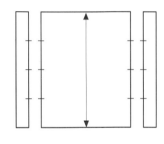

Cut the side borders to this length. If you are working on a table, don't allow the quilt top to hang and stretch over the edges of the table. Mark the center and quarter points of the quilt top and side borders.

Match pins, adding more as needed to secure, and ease where necessary. Sew with the border on the bottom so you can make sure the line of stitching does not cut off any points of the patchwork. Also make sure that the seams remain in the direction they were pressed.

Repeat for the top and bottom borders, measuring through the center of the quilt from side to side, including the borders you just added.

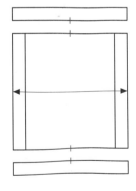

I do not miter the plain borders on these quilts because I think the mitered seam at a 45° angle looks funny with the 60° angles of the patchwork. Blunted corners are easier to keep square, too.

Using Pieced Borders

After browsing through hundreds, if not thousands, of quilt photos, I found that most quilts based on the equilateral triangle have plain borders or no borders at all. I rarely found a pieced border. Could it be that we are uncomfortable with the way a pieced border looks on these quilts because the edges of the design are not identical? That may be part of it, but I believe it also is because we think they require a bit of work to get them to fit properly. I hope that understanding the mystery of how to get them to fit will inspire you to try one.

If you would like to add a pieced border, keep to the same scale that you used in the quilt top. For good design, repeat the colors and shapes found in the central portion of the quilt. Refrain from using squares, circles, and appliqué.

You can design borders either lengthwise or crosswise on the equilateral-triangle graph paper, but you cannot draw the same border on adjacent sides. This is the biggest obstacle to planning the border. To repeat the border on adjacent sides and have four matching corners, you will need to cut and paste all four borders.

Miter the corners of a pieced border. In this way, you won't have to draft a special corner unit to make the corners look identical. Decide at what point in the design the corner will miter. You can do this while you are cutting and pasting at the design stage. View a sketch of the border folded at various points, or use a single mirror tile held at a 45° angle to the border.

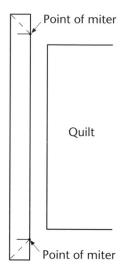

Mirror

Estimate the length of the pieced borders, based on your quilt diagram, then add 2½ times the width of the border to allow for the miter. For example, if the estimated length is 60" and the border is 2" wide, add 5" to the total border length to equal 65".

Borders for opposite sides of the quilt should be the same length. Adjust them if necessary.

Once you have made the borders, measure the length of each border along the inside edge from the point of the miter at one end of the border to the point of the miter at the other end.

Point of miter

Quilt

Point of miter

Spacer Strips

If you have chosen the perfect miter points to make your pieced border look stunning, but the length from miter point to miter point is longer than the length of the quilt, don't despair. There is a way to resolve this. For a perfect fit, add a spacer strip between the quilt top and the borders to get the border to miter at the desired point.

Spacer strips are usually cut from background fabric and inserted between the quilt top and pieced border. There is no standard formula for calculating their width; each set of spacer strips varies from quilt to quilt. For complete directions for calculating widths of spacer strips, see the "Triplicity" quilt plan on pages 66–67.

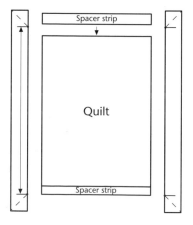

Spacer strip

Quilt

Spacer strip

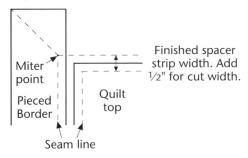

Miter point
Pieced Border
Finished spacer strip width. Add ½" for cut width.
Quilt top
Seam line

Do not sew the borders to the quilt until all of them have been made and measured, and all necessary spacer strips have been added.

> ### NOTE:
> *You may need to add spacer strips to the top and bottom only, or to the sides only.*

MITERING CORNERS

When adding the border to the quilt, match the centers, corners, and quarter points. Sew all four borders to the quilt top, stopping and backstitching ¼" from the corner to allow for the miter. For successful mitered or set-in seams, make sure the stitching comes up to but does not extend into the seam allowance. An open-toe presser foot for the sewing machine makes this step easier.

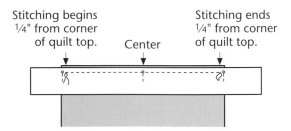

Stitching begins ¼" from corner of quilt top.
Center
Stitching ends ¼" from corner of quilt top.

With right side up, pin one edge of the quilt top to the ironing board to support the weight. Fold the end of the border that lies lengthwise on the ironing board at a 45° angle to the adjacent border, matching the border design along the fold. Make sure the corner is square; check the angle with the 45° angle on your ruler. Press the fold.

Pin it together along the fold and remove it from the ironing board.

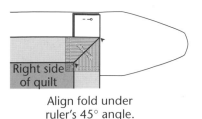

Right side of quilt

Align fold under ruler's 45° angle.

Carefully repin on the back with right sides together. If necessary, use a ruler and draw a pencil line on the fold. Machine baste along the fold. Stitch just to the seam allowance, not across it. Check that the corner design matches and adjust if necessary. When you are satisfied, stitch the seam, backstitching at the beginning and end of the seam. Trim the excess border, leaving a ¼"-wide seam allowance. Press this seam open.

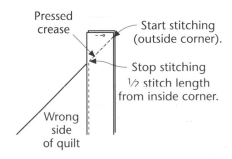

Pressed crease
Start stitching (outside corner).
Stop stitching ½ stitch length from inside corner.
Wrong side of quilt

If a pieced border places bias at the outside edges of the quilt, stabilize the bias by adding a plain border strip cut along the straight of grain *after* the pieced borders have been added to the quilt.

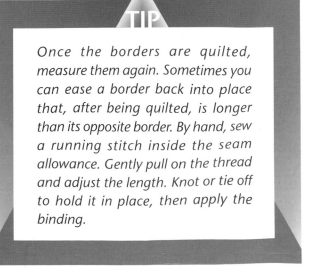

> ### TIP
> *Once the borders are quilted, measure them again. Sometimes you can ease a border back into place that, after being quilted, is longer than its opposite border. By hand, sew a running stitch inside the seam allowance. Gently pull on the thread and adjust the length. Knot or tie off to hold it in place, then apply the binding.*

FINISHING THE QUILT

BASTING

Basting temporarily holds the three layers of the quilt together during the quilting process. Basting prevents the layers from shifting and twisting and prevents puckers in the quilt. Mark all the necessary quilting designs before you baste. If you are using a temporary marker, mark the quilt after it is basted. Use the sample block to test the markers for ease of removal.

The type of basting to use depends on how it will be quilted. For a hand-quilted quilt, baste with thread. For machine quilting, I recommend pin basting. A #2 safety pin holds the layers securely and is easiest to handle. Place pins every 3" to 4" apart.

The larger the quilt, the larger the area you need for basting. Many quilters baste on a table or the floor. Often, quilt shops allow their customers to use a classroom table when it's not in use.

I like to use a basting frame. I can stand up instead of crawling on my hands and knees, and I get nice, smooth backs with equal tension in all areas of the quilt. Repositioning the quilt during basting can result in different tensions across the quilt. I use a basting frame for both pin basting and thread basting.

Make a basting frame from 1" x 2" x 8' lengths of lumber and staple a folded muslin strip to one edge of each of the four boards. C-clamps, available at hardware stores, hold the frame together at the corners. Use a chair at each corner to temporarily prop up the frame.

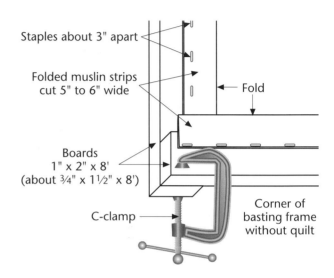

Staples about 3" apart

Folded muslin strips cut 5" to 6" wide

Fold

Boards 1" x 2" x 8' (about ¾" x 1½" x 8')

C-clamp

Corner of basting frame without quilt

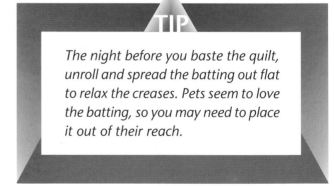

TIP

The night before you baste the quilt, unroll and spread the batting out flat to relax the creases. Pets seem to love the batting, so you may need to place it out of their reach.

To attach the quilt to the frame, position the boards so that any board longer than the edge of the quilt will be out of the way when the frame is set on end. Pin the backing, wrong side up, to the muslin on the frame. Start pinning on the board that will eventually sit on the floor. Stretch the backing taut and square as you pin.

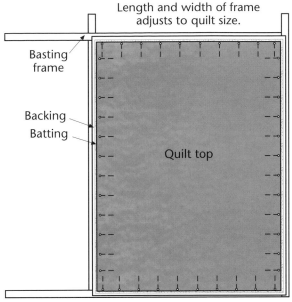

Length and width of frame adjusts to quilt size.

Basting frame

Backing

Batting

Quilt top

Rest this end on floor.

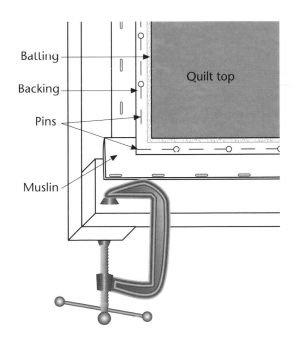

Batting

Backing

Pins

Quilt top

Muslin

Spread out the backing, the batting, then the quilt top, right side up. The backing and batting should be at least 2" larger than the quilt top on all sides. Use a few pins around the perimeter of

the quilt to hold the three layers together as you baste.

Begin basting from the top edge, which will be out of reach when the frame is upright. Stitch rows of basting 5" to 6" apart, with 1"- to 2"-long basting stitches. Baste horizontal rows, then the first part of the vertical rows in the order indicated in the diagram below. When you can no longer reach across the quilt comfortably, have someone help you move the frame from the chairs to prop it against a wall. Once the frame is standing against the wall, you may begin to notice gravity at work, making the quilt top sag. Working with gravity, start basting from the top to the bottom, following the general order for basting rows 4–10 (or more if needed) given in the illustration below.

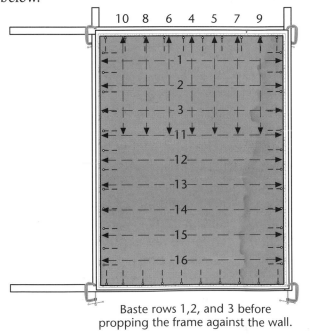

Baste rows 1, 2, and 3 before propping the frame against the wall.

After finishing the vertical rows, continue basting the horizontal rows, working from the center to each side. When the basting is completed, remove it from the frame. Turn the edge of the backing over the edge of the quilt and baste it in place to prevent the batting from shredding as you quilt.

QUILTING

Hand quilting can be done in your lap, in a quilting hoop, or on a quilting frame. To hand quilt, you need quilting needles, quilting thread, a thimble, and scissors or thread snips.

Begin by knotting the thread about ½" from the end. Insert the needle through the top layer of the quilt only, ½" in front of where you wish to begin stitching. Tug at the thread to pop the knot into the batting.

With the flat end of the thimble, push the needle through all three layers, taking tiny, even stitches. Do not hold the needle with finger and thumb while taking stitches. Try to get three to four stitches on the needle before pulling it through. Use the thumb of the hand on top of the quilt to help control the stitch length by placing it in front of the needle. Use the hand underneath the quilt to help push the needle back to the front.

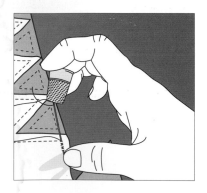

End by making a knot close to the fabric and inserting the needle back into the same hole where the last stitch came out. Travel between the layers a needle's length and come out on top. Gently pop the knot between the layers. Clip the threads close to the top. If the quilting ends near a seam, insert the needle again and travel one more inch before clipping the thread.

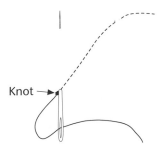

Knot →

When quilting is completed, do not trim the excess batting and backing yet. You will do this after attaching the binding.

Machine quilting provides a quicker way to secure the layers. I recommend pin basting before machine quilting. For straight stitching, loosen the top tension slightly and use an even-feed foot. For fancy patterns, drop the feed dogs and use a darning foot. Practice free-motion quilting on a layered scrap of fabric, batting, and backing before attempting it on your quilt.

Many excellent books and classes are available on the subject of hand and machine quilting to help you perfect your quilting skills. Refer to *Loving Stitches* by Jeana Kimball for hand quilting, and *Machine Quilting Made Easy* by Maurine Noble (both from That Patchwork Place).

BINDING

Bind the quilt after completing the quilting. Cut the number of 2½"-wide strips necessary to finish the quilt. Cut each end of the strips at a 45° angle. Join all the strips end to end as shown and press seams open. This diagonal seam distributes the bulk of the seam allowances for a smoother binding. Fold and press the strip in half lengthwise, wrong sides together. Press under ¼" at one end of the binding.

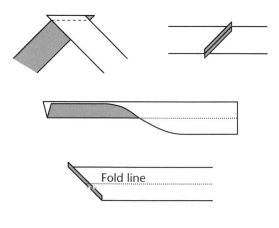

Fold line

Using a ¼"-wide seam allowance, start stitching about 3" from the end of the binding, beginning about 20" from the corner of the quilt. Sew through both layers of binding and all three layers of the quilt. Keep the edges of the binding even with the edge of the quilt top. Do not pin the binding to the quilt. Stop stitching ¼" from the corner and backstitch. Clip threads.

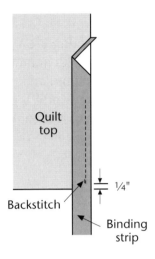

Turn the quilt and fold the binding away from the quilt as shown, then fold it back in place along the next edge. Keep the raw edges of the binding and the quilt top even all the way out to the corner. The extra fabric will form a perfect mitered corner when the binding turns the corner correctly. Stitch from the fold to within ¼" of the next corner and repeat these steps until all corners are sewn.

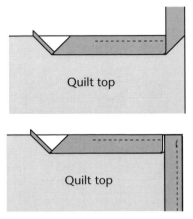

When you reach the beginning of the binding, cut the remaining piece at a 45° angle and tuck the end inside the beginning. Complete the seam.

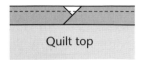

Trim the batting and backing so that when the binding is folded to the back, the batting fills the binding. Trim the two layers only about ⅛" wider than the quilt top.

Turn the binding to the back of the quilt so the folded edge covers the row of machine stitching. Blindstitch firmly in place with thread that matches the binding. At each corner, fold the binding to form a miter. Sew the miter closed on the front and back so the corners look neat.

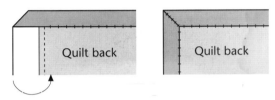

Be sure to sign and date your completed quilt.

About The Author

Resources

Order ClearView™ Triangles and equilateral-triangle graph paper from:

ClearView™ Triangle
8311 180th St. SE
Snohomish, WA 98290-4802 USA
Phone: 360-668-4151
Fax: 360-668-6338

Order equilateral-triangle graph paper from:

Lubisco Studios
12 The Arbor Way
Wayside, NJ 07712 USA
Phone: 908-918-1258
Fax: 908-775-5350

Gayle Bong has been an avid designer and quilter since 1981. In 1988, she began teaching classes on the art of quilting, specializing in adapting the latest rotary-cutting techniques to 60° shapes. Always intrigued by geometric design, the 60° angle caught her attention when she realized the potential it offered for new designs. Her first book, *Infinite Stars,* which converts traditional square blocks into stars, continues to dazzle quilters. Gayle has also contributed to the "What if? Design Challenge" column, a regular feature in *Traditional Quiltworks* magazine.

Gayle lives with her husband, Mark, and daughter, Lisa, in rural Elkhorn, Wisconsin, where she enjoys the peaceful life in the country. She is the founder and an active member of the Crazy Quilters and is a member of Wisconsin Quilters, Inc., and National Quilters Association. Gayle hopes many of the designs in her file will become more books to share with others.

YIELD CHART

The charts below show the number of pieces that can be cut from one strip, 40" long, and include sizes for pieces graphed at 1½" and 2" scale. All measurements include ¼"-wide seam allowances. For cutting instructions, see "60°-Angle Rotary Cutting," beginning on page 16.

Strip Width	Triangles per Strip	Half Triangles* per Strip
2¼"	29	58
2¾"	24	48
3¼"	21	42
3¾"	17	34
4¼"	16	32
4¾"	13	26
5¼"	13	26
5¾"	11	22
6¾"	9	18
7¼"	8	16
8¼"	7	14
8¾"	7	14
9¼"	6	12
9¾"	6	12
12¾"	4	8
13¼"	4	8

*These half triangles are mirror-image half triangles cut from bisected triangles.

Diamonds, Hexagons, and Gemstones (cut from diamonds)

Strip Width	No. per Strip
2"	16
2½"	13
3½"	9
4½"	7
5"	6
6½"	5
8½"	3
9½"	3
12½"	2

Half Triangles (from rectangles)

Strip Width	Length	No. per Strip
1⅝"	2¾"	30
1⅞"	3¼"	24
2½"	4¼"	18
3"	5¼"	14
3⅜"	5¾"	12
4¼"	7¼"	10
5⅜"	9¼"	8
7⅝"	13¼"	6
9⅜"	16¼"	4

Trapezoids

Strip Width	Height**	No. per Strip
2"	3¾"	12
2"	5¼"	8
2"	6¾"	6
2"	8¼"	4
2"	9¾"	4
2½"	4¾"	9
2½"	6¾"	6
2½"	8¾"	4
2½"	10¾"	3
2½"	12¾"	2
3½"	8¼"	5
3½"	9¾"	4
4½"	8¾"	5
4½"	10¾"	3
4½"	12¾"	3
5"	9¾"	4
5"	10¼"	4

**Trapezoid height refers to the line on the ClearView Triangle ruler at which the lower edge of fabric is placed.

Parallelograms

Strip Width	Length*	No. per Strip
2"	3½"	9
2"	5"	6
2"	6½"	5
2"	8"	4
2"	9½"	3
2½"	4½"	7
2½"	6½"	5
2½"	8½"	3
2½"	10½"	3
2½"	12½"	2

*Parallelogram length refers to the scale multiplied by the number of rows of graph paper.

Half Diamonds

Strip Width	Length	No. per Strip
1⅜"	4⅞"	15
1¹¹⁄₁₆"	5⅞"	12

Strip-Pieced Half-Diamond Units (cut from a panel of 8 strips)

Strip Width	Length	No. per Panel
1¾"	4"	60
2"	5"	49

That Patchwork Place Publications and Products